Dayspring MacLeod's new book on Dietrich Bonhoeffer is a welcome event. In these days of challenge, and the need for Christian fidelity, there is much in Bonhoeffer's story that reminds us of the ways faith can inspire courage and steadfast resolve—even in the face of greatest sacrifice. To read this intuitively-written book is to hear a call—to live a life of faith, courage, and resolve. May it find a wide, and well-deserved readership.

Kevin Belmonte
Historian; Author, *Beacon-Light:*
The Life of William Borden (1887-1913)

Christian Focus Publication's Hall of Faith biographies introduce a new generation of adult readers to a number of Christ's outstanding servants in the annals of the Christian Church. The lives, ministries, struggles and victories of these remarkable individuals provide inspiring and instructive examples for contemporary Christians and bring glory to God for His gracious work in and through His faithful, consecrated children. These biographies are highly accessible through their abbreviated length and engaging style. They will doubtless whet the appetite of many readers to learn more about these noteworthy Christians by reading the fuller accounts of their lives which these brief biographies recommend.

Vance Christie
Author, *David Livingstone:*
Missionary, Explorer, Abolitionist
and other Christian biographies

Dietrich Bonhoeffer

Dayspring MacLeod

CHRISTIAN
FOCUS

10 9 8 7 6 5 4 3 2 1

Copyright © Dayspring MacLeod 2023

Hardback ISBN: 978-1-5271-1052-6

ebook ISBN: 978-1-5271-1110-3

Previously published as *Dietrich Bonhoeffer: A Spoke in the Wheel*
(978-1-5271-0162-3) in the Trailblazer series.

Published by
Christian Focus Publications,
Geanies House, Fearn, Tain, Ross-shire,
IV20 1TW, Scotland, U.K.
www.christianfocus.com
email: info@christianfocus.com

Cover design by Laura K. Sayers
Printed by Gutenberg, Malta

Contents

INTRODUCTION

I was particularly pleased to hear that Christian Focus was re-issuing *A Spoke in the Wheel* for an older readership. Good stories appeal to children and adults alike, and Pastor Bonhoeffer comes alongside the reader as a lovable, humble, fascinating guide to a colourful cast of characters. As our understanding of history matures, those who encountered this story as children will see different shades in both the people and the war we encounter here - but the vivid sense of adventure and bravery only grows stronger as we grow up.

Indeed, the courage which is one of this story's main themes grows up along with us. As children we imagine ourselves in the place of Bonhoeffer and his friends, and we are sure we could have been just as strong in the face of Nazi opposition as they. As grown-ups, however, with a greater sense of our own weakness, their courage fills us with awe. We are aware of our own fear in the face of much lesser challenges, and we can only pray that the Lord will fill up our weakness with His strength. And, giving all glory to God, we know that this is indeed how the dear martyrs of World War Two, and throughout history, have overcome: by the blood of the Lamb, whose grace is abundantly sufficient for all who will ask for it.

But beyond the bravery which is so clearly one of the lessons we learn from Dietrich Bonhoeffer now, in another tumultuous and uncertain age, he teaches mature Christians another, and even harder, lesson. It is there in the very title of his best-known book, *The Cost of Discipleship*. It is there in the book's best-known quote:

> Cheap grace is the preaching of forgiveness without requiring repentance, baptism without church discipline, Communion without confession, absolution without personal confession. Cheap grace is grace without discipleship, grace without the cross, grace without Jesus Christ … Such grace is costly because it calls us to follow, and it is grace because it calls us to follow Jesus Christ. … Above all, it is costly because it cost God the life of his Son: "ye were bought at a price," and what has cost God much cannot be cheap for us.

In the six years since I wrote this book, I am thankful that God has continued to teach me. And one of the greatest lessons of my middle-aged life - at last - is to count the cost of discipleship. Do we examine ourselves to forsake not only all sins, not only all idols, but all distractions that take us away from the nearness of our Lord and the joy of the Spirit? Do we take captive all of our own thoughts for Him? Are we faithful in avoiding temptation, and persistent in actively seeking God's presence? Do we take up our cross daily to follow Him, or do we try to accept His gift of life without being crucified with Him? Are we external Christians only, or is Jesus Christ master of our thoughts, times, talents, and resources?

God's mastership of our lives, and the courage and strength we need to face the hardest circumstances, are not unrelated. It is as we trust Him, love Him, and willingly submit to Him that we are given what we need, day by day like the manna in the wilderness. Dependence on Christ alone is the key to all of it. We are never too old or too young for that lesson.

… You have been borne by me from before your birth, carried from the womb; even to your old age I am he, and to gray hairs I will carry you. I have made, and I will bear; I will carry and will save (Isa. 46:3b, 4 RSV).

Fear not, for I am with you; be not dismayed, for I am your God; I will strengthen you, I will help you, I will uphold you with my righteous right hand (Isa. 41:10 RSV).

At last the journey had come to an end.

Thirteen prisoners stumbled off the bus, stretching and blinking. The Nazi guards didn't have to push or threaten them: the prisoners were too tired and hungry after their three-day journey, all the way from Buchenwald Concentration Camp.

Most had been in prisons and concentration camps for years; cold, dingy, noisy places that smelled of death and sewer stink. Each one was a political prisoner, important in their own way, but they didn't look important. Dirty, half starved, and dressed in rags, most looked like any other inmates. Now they were led inside the only accommodation left in the tiny Bavarian village of Schonburg: the first floor of the school. The prisoners were shoved through a door and told to choose their beds.

When they turned and looked around, their mouths opened in surprise.

'I think we are in heaven,' said Pastor Bonhoeffer.

The other prisoners laughed. 'If heaven is where God is,' said a very proper English prisoner whom the guards called Herr Wolf, 'Pastor Bonhoeffer finds heaven everywhere – I've never met a man whose God was more real to him!'

But compared to the grey cells at Buchenwald, this did look like heaven. The room was a girls' dorm, full of light from the three large windows looking out at the forested valley, and plenty of soft feather beds covered with bright quilts. Above each bed was a little board where the girls wrote their names.

'Right,' said a middle-aged lady prisoner – who resembled nothing more than a headmistress – 'everyone choose their bed. My dear, let's make this young lady welcome, shall we?' She cast a meaningful look at her husband, a skinny but dignified old man, and together they shepherded a sloppy blonde girl to a bed at the far end of the room, where they could keep an eye on her.

'There's no need to police me,' the girl sulked. 'I'm not your daughter.'

'But I've never seen a young lady so in need of a mother,' the lady declared. 'War is brutal, but boarding men and ladies in the same room is really uncivilised. You know they're losing the war if it's come to this!'

The Englishman cleared his throat. 'I've a piece of chalk. We can write our names on the boards just as the little girls must do.'

'Ah, but not just our names,' said Dr Rascher, a young German with a little ginger moustache. 'Here we must celebrate our personalities. Nicknames for all!'

He first lighted on the bed of a Russian officer, a very young man dressed half in the uniform he'd worn to parachute into Germany years before, and half in civilian clothes that had replaced the worn-out bits. 'Vassily,' Rascher said jovially. The young man flinched at the loud

German voice, and made a great show of taking off his glasses and polishing them.

'What shall we call you? The Baby, for your innocent face? Simply the Russian? No, there is only one name we could use.' He went up to the Russian's chalkboard and wrote, 'The Nephew'.

The young man gave a little shrug of agreement. 'The only reason I am still here rather than executed with all my men.'

Pastor Bonhoeffer, standing nearby, looked puzzled.

'Did you not know?' Rascher asked. 'Vassily here is the nephew of Molotov – Stalin[1] rules Russia, and Molotov is his favourite person.'

'The Nephew,' Bonhoeffer agreed with a smile. Along with the others, he watched as Rascher skipped between each prisoner's bed, chalking in a nickname for each person: the Wolf, the Coward, the Statesman, the Blonde Bombshell, the Aristocrat, the Ambassador, the Matron.

'Now, Dr Rascher,' Bonhoeffer said, 'you are very good at observing others, but what about yourself?'

'Oh, I'm a doctor who prescribes laughter as the best medicine – so you can call me the Clown!' Rascher exclaimed, bowing low. 'But now we come to you, Pastor Bonhoeffer. How would you describe yourself?'

---

1. Josef Stalin was the communist dictator of Russia at this time. He was interested in Russian national pride but not in Russian people. One of his instructions was that any Russian soldier who turned back from battle or had been taken prisoner should be executed, both because being captured brought disgrace on the soldiers, and to show that it was absolutely necessary to beat the enemy – or pay the price. Molotov, a politician, was one of Stalin's most loyal supporters. The Nephew's real name was Vassily Kokorin.

Dietrich paused for a moment. How could he describe himself? He had no very defining physical characteristics. He had once been a stocky, muscular man, but now had the shrunken look of all long-term prisoners. He had a cheerful face, rimless glasses, and only a few strands of bright blond hair left on his wide forehead, though he was only thirty-six. He could describe himself as the Pianist, or the Academic, or the Radical, or the Man of Many Languages.

'I would suggest simply Brother Bonhoeffer,' he finally said.

'Dull! Something with more flair.'

'He's the Genius,' suggested the Aristocrat, who had known Dietrich's family before prison.

'He's the Man of God,' called out the Wolf.

'Both true, but unimaginative,' Rascher replied. 'I'll give him a name equally accurate, but one that no one will expect.' He reached up and, with undisguised glee, chalked in the words 'The Tyrannicide.' He made a sweeping gesture, as if presenting him anew to the other prisoners. 'Dietrich Bonhoeffer. The pastor who wanted to kill the Fuhrer!'

'That true?' asked the Wolf. 'If so, you're in good company here, old chap.'

'I was never going to plant a bomb or pull a trigger,' Dietrich said. 'I simply carried messages.' He turned to Rascher. 'But how did you know?'

'Ah well,' Rascher shrugged, 'it is not so long since I knew about everything connected with the Nazi government. I worked directly under Himmler, who organised the death camps.'

'Then why are you here?'

'The Fuhrer knows, dear Pastor Bonhoeffer,' Rascher replied with a short laugh. 'Only our dear good Fuhrer on high knows.'

'You're mocking me,' Dietrich said calmly.

'You say your God is good, but here you are, in the same place as me. What do you really know of your God and His goodness? Why are you here – if He is truly good and truly powerful?'

'Dear me,' the Wolf broke in hurriedly. 'I don't think I can take the destruction of the Christian faith on an empty stomach. I don't know whether it's the conversation or the starvation, but I'm feeling a trifle light-headed.'

He strode over to the door and banged as loudly as he could, keeping up the noise until one of the guards came to the door. 'Ah, my good man,' he said. 'What tidings of dinner?'

'I wish I knew,' the guard replied. 'Alas, Herr Wolf, there is nothing cooking either for you or us.'

'That will never do,' the Wolf replied briskly. 'Tell the commandant we wish to see him.'

'Yes, sir, but I don't know it will do much good.'

A moment later the commandant appeared in the room. 'Herr Wolf,' he said, with a nod to the rest of the prisoners. 'You made a complaint?'

'Not a complaint, sir, a request. We've been on the road for three days, and haven't had a good meal all that time. When's grub?'

The commandant shook his head apologetically. Wearied by six years of war, he was far from the image of a brutal Nazi officer. 'We have no food, not even for my men. This village is already billeting several dozen prisoners, and the mayor absolutely refuses to give us more out of their small store of provisions. There is a town an hour or two away, but we have no petrol to drive there and bring back food. I am doing everything I can.'

'This is a very serious matter,' the Wolf said gravely. 'We are political prisoners. That means we're due rations at double the rate of your soldiers. Starving us is illegal. You know the war is almost over, and I should hate for our governments to take stern measures against you for our treatment.'

The commandant sighed. 'Well, you will have to make a complaint about me, Herr Wolf, if you don't starve first. There's nothing I can do. The best thing is for you all to sleep. Perhaps by the time you awake we may have some breakfast for you.'

He backed out of the room and quickly turned the lock again.

'The way you speak to them!' the Coward said, with a mixture of horror and admiration. He looked near tears.

'I've been a prisoner for five and a half years – one learns to treat them simply as fellow officers,' the Wolf replied. 'Anyway, little good it did our tummies.'

'If I die before morning,' the Nephew said despondently, 'I suppose is better than die before Stalin's firing squad. I know he kills every soldier who was captured.'

'I shouldn't think it will come to that,' said the formidable lady, whose board read The Matron. 'Chins up, boys. I'll see what I can do. Herr Wolf, will you kindly get our guard's attention? I think I'd better make an excuse to go to the "little room".'

✎ CALLING ✎

The prisoners sat on their beds and chatted, waiting to hear news of the Matron's success. Dietrich went over to the Nephew, who was standing around between their two beds, looking depressed, as usual.

'I have a favour to ask you,' he said. 'I was wondering if you might take a stab at teaching me Russian.'

The Nephew gave him a thin smile. 'I can teach you, but will you ever use the language?'

'I expect I may have a chance, though not in Russia,' Dietrich replied. 'I gather that your soldiers are closing in on Berlin. No doubt there will still be one or two of them there after the war.'

'Maybe I teach you some words, but you never understand true Russian character,' the Nephew responded. 'You are preacher, yes? In my country we understand that man no longer needs God and no longer needs church.'

'What you think man needs is irrelevant,' Dietrich replied. 'God exists, and the church exists, and man is called to serve both.'[1]

---

1. This is a direct quote from Bonhoeffer.

'I not understand. Doctor Bonhoeffer' –
'Pastor.'

'Yes, yes. Pastor Bonhoeffer. You have good brain. Very intelligent man, and educated. Why then you study God, and not useful thing like science or economics?'

'Not out of any real interest in God, to begin with, and certainly not because I knew Him,' Dietrich replied. 'It was because of my own pride.'

And because he now had time, and because the Russian seemed interested, and because there was little else to do, he started to tell his story.

1915

Finally, it was Christmas Eve. For all the weeks of Advent, nine-year-old Dietrich and his twin sister Sabine had almost felt they were holding their breath. It was like that Christmas carol, *O Holy Night*: 'Long lay the world in sin and error pining, till he appeared, and the soul felt its worth.' During Advent the Bonhoeffer children were encouraged to think about their sin, the reason Jesus died to deliver them. They tried to long for the Messiah to come, just as Israel must have done. The whole of December felt like a long wait.

Finally Christmas Eve came. It was early evening, the last blue gleam of dusk dying away. Dietrich gazed at the chandelier overhead and listened to his mother's voice, full of awe and suspense, reading the Christmas story out of Luke.

Fear not: for, behold, I bring you good tidings of great joy, which shall be to all people. For unto you is born this day in the city of David a Saviour, which is Christ the Lord. And this shall be a sign unto you; Ye shall find the babe wrapped in swaddling clothes, lying in a manger. And suddenly there was with the angel a multitude of the heavenly host, praising God and saying, Glory to God in the highest, and on earth peace, goodwill toward men (Luke 2:10-14 KJV).

All day the scent of gingerbread had wafted up from the kitchen, and there was still a whiff of it in the air, mingling with the fresh pine branches decorating the mantelpiece. Dietrich's mouth watered and he glanced around the room, trying to distract himself from his rumbling tummy by looking at each well-known face: parents, brothers, sisters, and in the back, the maids with their white aprons catching the dim lamplight. He saw, from the corner of his eye, his father sneaking out of the room, and his heart leapt with excitement. Which of the presents he had requested from Saint Nicholas would be under the tree – the spinning top? The air rifle? The books?

His brother Walter, who was fourteen, gave the lightest of coughs, and Dietrich caught his eye and grinned, blushing to be caught daydreaming. Walter was a gentle soul and never reprimanded anyone, but he was so sweet-natured that he made all his little brothers and sisters want to be good too.

Mother closed the book. 'This is the day that God has made,' she said, the title of their first song.

The maids smiled and went to turn off all the lights, and in the dark, all the children's voices followed their mother's. It was quite a choir now: all the Bonhoeffer children had special musical gifts, and the oldest boys had deep voices to fill out the harmonies. Dietrich was only a boy, with a pure voice, higher than his sister's.

As they sang 'Silent Night,' a bell rang out. The children's voices faltered with excitement, and though they tried to keep singing, Mother laughed. 'All right, go on now. Happy Christmas!'

The doors were flung open and they rushed into the parlour, where the enormous tree was alight with bright flickering candles. The floor was covered with presents wrapped in shiny paper and big silk bows, but the children tried hard not to look at them, and went first to the nativity scene set up on the table. 'Christ is come!' At once all the waiting, the stillness of winter, and their own sins were forgotten. Christ had come, bringing light brighter than any Christmas tree.

1918

Nobody had really thought the Great War would last long enough for the Bonhoeffer boys to reach the age of joining the army. But it had been long and deadly and Germany was running out of young men.

The night before Walter left for training, the family held one of their dinners – a grand, formal, yet affectionate affair. Each Bonhoeffer had to give a recital or musical performance, and Dietrich set the words of a prayer to music as a gift for his brother. He was already a good singer and an even better pianist, and knew it. There was talk of sending him to the music conservatory, and Dietrich could picture himself on the stage of the Berlin Opera House, playing for thousands of faces. As he sang for Walter he took pleasure in his own voice, his own fingers moving across the keys. He was pleased to hear his voice break, a perfect show of emotion. What a performer!

'Thank you, Dietrich,' Walter said after the concert, carefully folding the sheet music Dietrich had presented to him. 'Your song means a lot to me, and your prayer means even more.'

In the morning the younger children hung around Walter's room, watching him get ready to go. He was already packed, but now he put the last few things into his rucksack: toothbrush, comb, Bible. There was a feeling of forced cheerfulness in the house, a heaviness the children could almost touch and smell, though there were no tears.

But at the train station, the steam engine's big wheels turned and Walter started to pull away, his head framed by the window, his arm outstretched toward home, toward the past – and Mother ran. She ran alongside the train, trying to keep up, her arm reaching out toward Walter, and she called, 'It's only space that separates us!'

'Of course it is,' thought Dietrich. 'What else could separate two people but space?'

The telegram came only two weeks later. And Dietrich learned what else could separate people: time. Walter would always remain seventeen, and yet, in Dietrich's mind, would always be his big brother, even when he himself was twice that age. Walter had died of an infected wound. It seemed that being a soldier was not quite as glamorous as Dietrich had imagined.

At the funeral, Mother was as calm and serene as ever. She sang the hymns in a loud, clear voice, and nodded along with the sermon about how the pains and sorrows of this life are nothing compared to the joys of heaven. But in the months, then years, to come, she could barely get out of bed. She stayed with friends so that her children wouldn't see her break down with grief.

On one of his visits to her, Dietrich asked, 'Why did Walter have to die?'

Mother's eyes filled with tears. 'It's all right to wonder. But I don't suppose we'll know until we reach heaven.'

And Dietrich thought, 'Yes, we will. I will explain.'

1945

'It was not an easy thing to tell my family that I was going to become a theologian,' Dietrich told the Nephew. 'To my brothers and sisters I might as well have decided to study fairy tales. They were all ambitious – all successful too, the older ones. One was a famous scientist; another the main lawyer for Lufthansa, Germany's national airline; two of my sisters married important lawyers. Most of them thought the Bible was just a long fantasy story that couldn't be real.'

'They must be disappointed when you told them you were going into the church.'

'Yes, all except Mother. They used to test me by asking me all sorts of impossible questions, though I was only fourteen and didn't know much yet. I had more questions than any of them!'

'It is very useless thing,' said the Nephew, 'someone who can only ask questions and not answer any.'

'Yes, but in a way I was more ambitious than my siblings. They only sought to explain science; I wanted to explain life. I intended to master the philosophy of God, and make myself a great name doing so.'

'And did you?'

'No,' Dietrich said, 'because it mastered me instead. I tried to use Jesus' cross to benefit myself and my own pride – but I had not reckoned on the power of God.'

He held up his worn Bible, which was always on his bed or in his hand. 'Mother gave this to me when I was confirmed in the church. It was Walter's. He was a humble man. I am still learning to become one, too.'

∽ TEACHING ∽

Dietrich was a quick learner, but he had barely heard any Russian, and it turned out to be a difficult language, full of sounds that didn't exist in German or English or any of the other languages he spoke.

'Zdravstvuyte,' he said, for the thirtieth time. The Nephew had repeated it over and over, written it down in simple syllables that Dietrich could sound out, and explained what sound was made by each of the Russian letters. Now Dietrich could just barely say it – 'Hello.'

The Nephew shrugged. 'Better. Now you can make the word, but still you cannot make the accent. You sound like German speaking Russian.'

Dietrich took his glasses off and rubbed away the two little dents they left on his nose. 'Maybe it's time for a break.'

The Nephew laughed. 'What is harder? Russian or this – teo – theo –'

'Theology,' Dietrich smiled. 'I don't know that theology is so very difficult. It's just a matter of knowing the Bible. Once you've read and understood the Bible, you should be able to make it simple enough to teach to children.'

'Da, like history. So many facts to memorise. So little use for it.'

'Oh no, Vassily. Like history, it only matters if you understand why, not just what happened. And that was one of the first classes I ever taught – on understanding.'

1927

'So,' Dietrich's professor said, 'you've finished your doctoral dissertation already.'

'Well, it needs a bit of polishing,' Dietrich replied cheerfully. 'But most of it is in place.'

The professor nodded at the golden-haired twenty-one-year-old in front of him. 'What is the Church?' he murmured, flipping through the pages of the manuscript. 'You've come up with a good academic study, but perhaps it's time for some pastoral experience. Do you have a church?'

Dietrich shook his head. 'My mother loves God, but my father is an agnostic. We don't go anywhere regularly.'

'I see. Well, we're going to find a congregation where you can do some teaching. You can't be ordained until you're twenty-five – you may as well do something worthwhile in the meantime!'

Dietrich was sent to the parish church in Grunewald, a rich and educated part of Berlin. He would preach once in a while, but his real task was teaching Sunday School. He found that he loved spending time with the children, and he and his younger sister Susi liked to take them on outings to the zoo or picnics at the Tiergarten, Berlin's vast park. He spent so much time with them that his father, the respected psychiatrist Karl Bonhoeffer, asked if he was giving up theology to look after children.

'In all seriousness, Father, I've been wondering if I should be a pastor instead of a professor,' Dietrich told him. 'Theology exercises my mind, but teaching these children is so rewarding.'

'Dietrich, you have too much brain to spend all your time telling children Bible stories.'

'On the contrary – I enjoy the challenge of explaining even the most profound biblical concepts in such a way that children can understand and enjoy them. I'm not just telling them about Noah's Ark, I'm explaining how the Ark foreshadows Jesus as the one true vessel in which we can enter and be saved from destruction!'

His father, the agnostic, shrugged his shoulders. It was hard to argue with Dietrich – he was too good at it. 'I suppose you will use your brain in whatever you do.'

But his father's concern made Dietrich think, and the questions that the older children asked him made him think even more.

'Herr Bonhoeffer, we've learned much about the Bible, but do you really expect us to believe it?' asked one of the teenage boys. 'Even the professors at the university only teach the Bible as history or literature. Do you really expect educated, thinking people to believe in God and the devil and angels?'

'Not everyone is like our Berlin professors,' Dietrich told them. 'There's a Swiss professor called Karl Barth who's a real radical – he insists that even academics can and should believe in God!'

'But what about evolution?' asked one.

'And what about the gods the Germans worshipped hundreds of years ago?' asked another. 'How do we know our religion is true and theirs wasn't?'

'Or the Muslims?'

'Or the Catholics?'

'And why should we pray if God already knows everything that will happen?'

'Was Jesus really God, or just a Jewish teacher who was executed by the Romans?'

'Let me think,' Dietrich said.

The next week he sent invitations to the most curious boys in the class, a group of fourteen and fifteen-year-olds who were as full of questions as Dietrich had been at their age. The Thursday Circle would meet for an hour and a half every week at the Bonhoeffers' home and discuss a different topic.

Though Dietrich was the teacher, researching the topic and leading the discussion, he treated the teenagers like grown-ups, using the same terms and arguments as if he were speaking to fellow students at the university. He took them to the opera and led a discussion of Wagner, and took them to the art museum to talk about the faith of great artists like Durer and Rembrandt.

Many of the students were Christian Jews.

✑ EQUALITY ✑

Dietrich and the Nephew were interrupted by a great deal of commotion in the room: a clatter, and a great rushing of feet, and cheers. But Dietrich barely even registered these things, because they were all drowned out by one thing – the smell. Food! After two years in prison, Dietrich had developed a sixth sense for food. Almost involuntarily, he leapt to his feet and, along with the Nephew, joined the mass of shouting prisoners surrounding the basin of steaming boiled potatoes. A flushed, smiling housekeeper was lugging them to the table, all the male prisoners trying to help her carry the food faster. 'What a shame, bringing you here with no way to feed you! Why, when this poor lady found me on her way to the toilet and told me how hungry you were, I simply had to find something!'

'Three cheers for the Matron!' Rascher cried, but by then everyone was digging into the potatoes, too busy blowing and munching and gulping down coffee to cheer.

'When I think of the golden schnitzel and fried potatoes with bacon that my wife and I ate from China plates in our home in the Netherlands, I can't quite believe myself tearing into a boiled potato with so much delight,' the Wolf said to Dietrich.

'No butter, no salt, no meat – but after three days without food, I think it's the best thing I ever ate,' Dietrich agreed.

'Still can't say the same for this fake coffee,' the Wolf said, and both men laughed.

'Is it ungrateful to wish for a few more potatoes?' Rascher asked, walking up to them. His potato was already gone and he was licking his fingers.

'I'd say it's pretty natural, when you're still as hungry as ever,' the Spy replied.

'I suppose I'll try to focus on sleep,' Rascher sighed. 'I haven't had a bed that comfortable in months.'

'Two years for me,' said Dietrich.

'Five and counting,' chimed in the Wolf. 'I'm going to get some more of that terrible coffee first – see you anon, chaps.'

He moved away, and Rascher held up his cup. 'Well, cheers.'

Dietrich tapped his cup to the doctor's, but he looked thoughtful, and put it down again without drinking. 'I know who you are,' he said.

The doctor slurped down the last of his coffee. 'Yes?'

'You were at Dachau. You're the one who came up with the gas chambers to kill the Jews.'

'Yes, what did you think?' Rascher asked excitedly. 'Very efficient, no? Saved the army millions of bullets.'

'But then you are responsible for millions of deaths,' Dietrich replied.

'Those people were going to die anyway – there was simply no longer room for them in our country.

When you think about it, gas was the kindest way to do it. They just thought they were getting a shower! It would have been like going to sleep. Himmler was so pleased they weren't suffering – he's not a monster, you know.'

'The poor souls did not deserve to die,' Dietrich said. 'And I know too about the experiments you performed on some of them. Freezing them to death. Putting them into pressure chambers.'

'And discovered many things that will help our pilots and explorers,' Rascher shot back. 'This was important research that will benefit the whole world. So what if a few criminals had to die!'

'In great suffering and pain,' Dietrich replied. 'And all for the crime of being Jewish, Romanies, or simple-minded.'

'They were not useful members of society.'

'And that is for you to decide, not God?'

'The Fuhrer decided!' Rascher snapped. 'Anyway, you traitor – you deserted your country when she needed you the most. Germany is at war! She has lost many men, she needs every resource she can get. The whole world is against her. And you betray her by trying to overthrow the government! Why not worry about the whole of Germany rather than just the criminals and the weak?'

'The reason I have compassion for the Jews and Romanies – all those who are different – is because I have known and lived among those who are different. I have seen the injustice and the suffering.'

'You have lived among Jews?' Rascher asked with a smirk.

'Jews? Oh, I have Jews in my family, in my church, and among my colleagues. It was nothing new to be among Jews. No – I lived among blacks.'

1930

As the ship pulled into New York Harbour, Dietrich could hear many languages from the passengers around him, crowding each other on the decks to get a better look at Manhattan. In German, English, Spanish, Italian – all of which Dietrich spoke – he could hear the same thing: 'Look! So big. So new. So high. We are here. America!'

They sailed past the great green lady with her torch raised high above her head. The tourists in her crown waved and shouted at the ship, and the children on board waved and shouted back, though it was too far for them to hear each other. The great glass and steel monsters on land towered up to the sky, the Chrysler and Empire State Buildings straining up to see which could brush the highest cloud, each of them topped by a mass of unfinished girders. The upper floors teemed with crews of men stacking one storey on top of another. After the stately old stone buildings of Berlin, it reminded Dietrich of the Bible story of the Tower of Babel. An ancient city had decided to build a tower that would reach up to heaven itself. To put an end to their prideful plan, God had set them all speaking different languages so that they could no longer understand each other, and so they had scattered over the earth. With its huge buildings, its pride and its countless languages, New York seemed like a modern-day Babel.

Union Seminary, where Dr Dietrich Bonhoeffer was teaching for a year, felt as if it had the same aims. They were there to talk about God, not to learn how to follow Him better. Dietrich didn't mind that – he was an academic, not a missionary – but this American school seemed lazy and unoriginal. Even worse, the church that most of the students attended didn't take God seriously at all. It was more like a social club that organised lots of functions, from charity auctions to tea parties and even bowling, but little Bible study or real preaching. It was just a place for decent, educated, rich white people to get together.

So when a black student, Frank Fisher, invited Dietrich along to a service at Abyssinian Baptist Church in Harlem, he was happy to accept. Dietrich had run Sunday School classes for poor students in Barcelona during a summer of ministry there, so he was used to being outside his comfortable, middle-class circle. He was not, however, used to being the only white face in a sea of black ones. He stuck close to Frank. The other church members stared, but they were all friendly. Frank introduced him to friends and pastors who shook his hand and asked him how he liked America.

As they sat down, a group of young girls looked at them and giggled. 'No offence, Dr Bonhoeffer,' Frank grinned, 'but I think you're the whitest man they've ever seen!'

Dietrich laughed. 'I do feel quite the centre of attention. I guess this is how you feel all the time in white neighbourhoods.'

Frank's face fell. 'Not quite, sir.'

'What do you mean?'

'Let's go to lunch sometime, and you'll see.' He pointed up to the pulpit. 'It's starting.'

There was music like Dietrich had never heard before. He was used to sublime operas and concertos, but the black gospel music made his heart roll like a stone from a tomb. The songs often started with sorrow and then rose with volume and harmony and hope as the choir sang about heaven and the Jesus who was always there for them through their sorrows on earth. They clapped and shouted and danced, and so did the congregation. They all seemed to be singing in perfect harmony, and Dietrich's mouth fell open. He was forgotten, unseen, with everyone's eyes on the Lord. The hair on his arms and neck stood on end and he found himself clapping along without even being aware of it. Like the rest of the worshippers, he forgot all about himself and only remembered the Jesus he was singing about.

'That was incredible!' he whispered excitedly to Frank as the song ended with a great final shout. 'Is it always like this?'

Frank smiled. 'Wait till you hear the preaching.'

Dr Powell was an old, white-haired man, but everything about him showed quiet power: the way he stood, the dignity of his ministerial robe, the seriousness of his voice that soared effortlessly over the congregation.

'Are any of you poor?' the pastor asked.

Most hands went up. 'Yes, pastor!'

'How many of you know what it is to mourn?'

'Right here, Reverend! I do!'

'Are any of you meek? Do you hunger and thirst after righteousness? Good! You see, there are no promises for those who are already rich and full and happy with only the things this world has to offer. Why is it so hard for a rich man to enter the kingdom of heaven? Because he doesn't need for anything! Does he know anything about poverty and mourning and meekness? Well, what does he cry out to Jesus to deliver him from, then? And if you don't need washing, if you don't need feeding, if you don't need saving, how can you ever love Jesus?'

Dietrich couldn't even breathe. He had never wanted for a thing in his life. He had never asked Jesus for anything. He could preach, but he didn't know how to pray. He believed in God, but he hadn't known he needed to be saved.

'You can't come to Jesus,' said the preacher, and it was as if the words spoke only into Dietrich's ear, 'unless you are poor, and mourning, and meek, and hungry. And every human soul on earth is these things, if they can only see it. Helpless as a baby. Every soul needs Jesus.'

The congregation erupted in an ecstatic furore. 'Yes! Hallelujah!'

Unannounced, they launched into another song. The others leapt to their feet, but Dietrich was rooted to his chair. He had studied God for eight years, and in his mind he believed that Jesus really existed and had really died on the cross for people's sins. He understood all the big words: redemption, atonement, sanctification. But suddenly his heart understood that God's power was real, that Jesus had died for him, that Jesus now demanded that Dietrich should no longer live his own way but give his all to Christ.

On the way out of the church, Dietrich shook Dr Powell's hand.

'We don't get many of you here,' Powell said.

'Whites?'

Dr Powell grinned. 'Union Seminary men. The gospel isn't usually your style.'

'Dr Powell, I have a little experience,' Dietrich replied slowly. 'Do you think Abyssinian could use a new Sunday School teacher?'

'I'm sure we could put you to work!'

As he beamed at Dr Powell, Dietrich felt as if he had been granted a special privilege: his first real act of service to God.

1945

'Well,' Rascher said, 'it sounds like your primitive friends were a pleasant enough bunch.'

'Primitive?' Dietrich asked. 'Herr Doctor, having dark skin does not mean they just emerged from the jungle. Frank taught me far more than I ever taught him.'

'Like what?'

'That Jesus was real.' Dietrich held out his hands, smiling at the memory. 'There I was, already a doctor of theology at an incredibly young age, from a deeply refined European family. And it took that black student to teach me that Jesus was real. Do you know how?'

'Clearly not,' Rascher said.

'I had to look up at Jesus, from below. From a position of humility. Of need. Of suffering. Up until then, I had rather looked down at Jesus, as a subject to be mastered and explained. I was a theologian but not a Christian. I had to learn to obey.'

'Well, perhaps you would explain one thing to me about your precious obedience. Doesn't your Bible also say to obey all those in authority over you?'

'Yes.'

'Then how can you justify yourself in plotting against the Fuhrer?'

'I can't justify myself,' Dietrich said. 'For that or anything else.'

The doctor's brow furrowed. 'What?'

'God decides what is right. I am only acceptable if He accepts me. And He can only do so because of what Jesus has done, not because of anything I've done. When He asks me one day to justify myself, I'll just point at Jesus. What will you do?'

HOW TO TEACH THEOLOGY

After Rascher stomped off, the Wolf sidled back up to Dietrich. 'What was all that about?' he asked.

'Oh, I gave him some unwanted pastoral advice. I'm not sure of the chances of his coming round to it.'

'What was the advice?'

'Repent, for the Kingdom of God is near. That was roughly it.'

The Wolf laughed. 'I've been watching you for the past few days. You're good at finding exactly what people don't want to hear, and telling them.'

'I prefer to think of it as telling people what they need to hear.'

The Wolf crossed his arms. 'I'm sure you've been watching me too. What do I need to hear?'

'When I know, you can be sure I'll tell you!'

'You may be required to shout. I'm not very good at hearing things I'd rather not.'

'Shouting is not the way to be heard,' Dietrich told him. 'That was a lesson I learned early in my career.'

1932

After a year of ministry in Barcelona and another in New York, Dietrich was sent to teach another confirmation class in Berlin. This one was across the city in Wedding, one of the poorest areas. Confirmation was meant to show that the children understood and accepted all the great truths of the Bible and were ready to be full members of the church, but most of these children's parents only sent them to keep them out of the house and off the street.

Dietrich arrived for his first day of class looking forward to teaching children again. He had loved his Sunday School classes in Grunewald, Barcelona and New York, and hoped this would be equally rewarding. Outside the building he was met by a furious and exhausted old minister.

'You're the new fellow?' he asked, nearly shouting. There was an incredible noise coming from the room, two floors above, where the children were gathered for class.

'Yes, I'm Bonhoeffer!'

'Well, you're welcome to them. Take my advice and don't spare the rod – punishment is the only language they understand.'

Dietrich ignored that. 'What have they learned so far?'

'Learned?' The man gave a hollow laugh and led the way into the building.

Dietrich was hit first by a bit of orange peel, then a damp shred of smelly cheese. He felt something crunch under his foot and found a piece of chalk crushed under his shoe. Looking up the stairwell, he saw a couple of dozen dirty faces jeering down at him, and narrowly missed having his glasses knocked off by a stale crust of bread. The old minister was shouting as he stamped up the stairs. Dietrich clenched his jaw and climbed steadily on.

They reached the top of the stairs and the minister herded the children into the classroom, distributing several smacks to encourage them along. 'Sit down! Quiet! This is your new teacher, Dr Bonhoeffer' –

'BON! BON! BON! BON!' The children slammed their hands on their desks in time with their new teacher's nickname.

The minister turned to Dietrich. 'They're all yours,' he said, and made his retreat, slamming the door behind him.

Dietrich stood with his hands in his pockets and silently looked at his new class. Boys sitting on chairs. Boys sitting on desks. Boys standing on desks. Boys hanging out the window shouting to people outside. Boys shoving each other. All the boys were dirty and noisy.

Dietrich reflected. The old teacher had told him to use physical punishments, but clearly those had not worked. He would have to try something else. He thought about what had worked for him as a high-spirited boy. What had induced him to sit down and behave? Stories.

'During the year I spent in New York City,' he began quietly, 'I lived among the whites, but I worshipped and often spent time with the black community. They were poor but hardworking, mostly living in one crowded but vibrant part of the city, called Harlem.'

Hardly anyone had heard him, but at this point one or two of the boys nearest him slid into chairs to listen.

'I had a black student called Frank, and one day we decided to go out to lunch. There was a diner near the seminary that sold schnitzel, and I wanted Frank to taste a little something from Germany. Well, we walked into the diner, escaping the autumn heat – many restaurants in New York have artificial air conditioning, and it felt like walking into an icebox. It was wonderful. But as we looked around for empty chairs, suddenly all the other customers went silent. They were all staring at us. I felt as if I had a sign on my back or something.'

'Hey, quiet!' The front row was now full of boys. One of them threw a pencil at the noisy students in the back. 'We want to hear!'

Dietrich kept talking quietly. 'I thought perhaps they weren't used to new customers – maybe it was just a place for regulars. We went up the counter and a waitress came to see us. I ordered the schnitzel, but she just looked right at Frank and said' –

The boys leaned forward.

'"We're all out of fried chicken and watermelon".'

Nearly all the boys were paying attention now. 'What did that have to do with it?' one of them demanded. 'You asked for schnitzel!'

'Exactly what I pointed out to her. She told me they only had one schnitzel left. "Give it to my friend," I said, "and I'll have a hamburger." So she told me' –

Now all the boys were listening.

' – that there was no schnitzel at all.'

'She doesn't sound like a great waitress,' a boy called out.

'I was flabbergasted,' Dietrich said. 'Finally she came to the point. She said, "Look, you can have anything you want. The kitchen don't have nothing for your black boy here." That's exactly how she said it – some

Americans talk that way, you see. Can you imagine such a thing happening in Germany, refusing service to a person because of their race?'

The boys were altogether silent.

'So what did I do?' Dietrich asked. 'I told her we'd find a more broad-minded restaurant, and stormed out along with Frank. I never went back, no matter how much I missed schnitzel.'

'So what?' asked one of the boys, bored. 'So you had to go to another restaurant.'

'Well, that was my plan. I asked Frank where we could go. And he told me every diner in that white neighbourhood would call him "boy" and offer him fried chicken and watermelon because they thought it was all blacks ate. He knew all the time what would happen when we walked in there. He wanted me to see for myself what it was like.'

'Did you ever get lunch?' someone called out.

'Yes. Luckily, hot dog stands serve everyone, even in New York! But I had a question for him. I wanted to know, if this was how white people treated him all the time, why he and his church had been so nice to me.'

'Why were they?' a boy in the front row asked.

'Because Jesus had taught them to love their enemies,' he replied. 'And their plan, the only way forward, was to win people over with kindness and humility. Whites had power to mistreat the blacks, but they couldn't force the blacks to react with hate.'

The room was silent except for the ticking of the clock.

'Class dismissed,' Dietrich said. 'If you behave well next time, I'll tell you another story about New York. Then we can start thinking about the catechism.'

'That was how I went on,' Dietrich said, 'telling them about New York, playing them songs from my collection of black gospel music, then reading to them some of the exciting and scary passages from Revelation. By that time they were willing to listen to anything I had to say. I took a flat in their poor area of Berlin, and told them they could come to see me any time. I had them over for dinner individually, and we had the most serious conversations about the Bible, faith, morality, whatever trials and heartaches they were going through. Once I had their trust and respect, they discovered they were positively hungry to talk about Jesus. Now that, in my opinion, is the best theology class I've ever taught.'

The Wolf smiled. 'So, Pastor Bonhoeffer, you can tame the wildest children and, I've heard, also entrance the greatest minds with your profound books. You can speak any number of languages. I think rather than the Tyrannicide, Rascher should have called you the Professor. But is it really true that other races were welcome in Germany not so long ago? It's hard to imagine when so many have been killed in concentration camps.'

'This is proof that hatred is not something natural to the German people,' Dietrich said sadly. 'The Nazis found threads of racism in the people – as there are in any nation – and pulled and pulled at these threads until they grew and ripped apart the very society they were part of. Yes, fifteen years ago a black man and a white man might have been friends in my country. Now, if two such were to walk into a restaurant together, not only would the black man be killed for his race, but the white man would be killed for being his friend. And perhaps, with all the work I have done for the Resistance, all my work against the Nazis, some of my most important work has been teaching children like these. Teaching them not that Nazis are bad, but that hatred is.'

'I only wish, my dear fellow, that I could say your work had been enough.'

Dietrich shook his head. 'How could one man's work ever be enough against such terrors? Ten years I have been devoted to this cause, to stopping this evil government. It may be that the day of judgment will dawn tomorrow; and in that case, I shall gladly stop working for a better future. But not before.'[1]

---

1. This is a quote from Bonhoeffer's essay 'After Ten Years'. He wrote it from prison to encourage his friends who were also resisting the government, sending it to them as a Christmas present.

∾ A LETTER HOME ᷃

It was nearly ten o'clock: lights out. The prisoners stalled for time like children, standing and chatting at each other's beds, trading books, taking turns in the toilet. But finally everyone was in their beds, and they had barely touched down on those beautiful feather pillows before their eyes clamped shut, too tired after all the day's excitement to stay open a minute longer. They might have stalled like children, but they also slept like children, worn out after too much travel and too much play.

They hardly registered the whine and zoom of the Allied planes overheard, the occasional far-off whizz and boom of bombs. These sounds were as natural to them now as crickets chirping or the hoot of an owl: a wartime lullaby.

Suddenly there was a loud crack, right there in the room. Everyone sat bolt upright. A bomb? A gunshot? Shocked silence gave way to shouted questions, and then, by the moonlight, everyone saw the man Rascher had called the Coward sitting foolishly on the ground, in a state of shock but otherwise unharmed.

'I say, are you all right, old fellow?' asked the Wolf. 'It looks like your bed's given way!'

Dietrich gave the Coward a hand up and pointed down at the mattress. 'See here, half the boards have been removed from beneath.'

'Another wartime ration, no doubt! The army needed more wood!'

They put the bed back together and the Coward reclined himself down again, rather more carefully this time. After a good laugh everyone else lay down too, only to hear another loud crack and find the Wolf on the floor. It was a few minutes before all the beds and all the prisoners were finally behaving themselves, and snores once more filled the air.

Dietrich didn't find it so easy to fall back to sleep this time. He was too wide-awake, perhaps distracted by the bombers, or simply by the gnawing in his stomach. After two years he was used to it, but it was sharp tonight. Which was louder, the planes or the hunger?

He wrote a letter in his head.

Dear Maria,

A peaceful day. With all the worrying you must do on my behalf, I wish you could have seen my merry little band today, the outlandish characters, the jokes, the kindness of one 'criminal' to another. Our temporary home is a girls' school – and what a view! A serene, forested valley; it seems to make you closer, you and the peace of your Pomeranian home. I hope you are back there now, just so that we will be looking at the same sort of view.

I still have my Bible and I opened it to 1 Thessalonians and saw the verse, 'You are in my heart to live and die with you.' That's what you are for me, always with me no matter my whereabouts or my circumstances. And to think there was a day when you thought of me as a stuffy, remote grown-up; when you refused to admit you felt anything for me, supposing that I must just think of you as a little sister; when you could not imagine calling me Dietrich instead of Pastor Bonhoeffer! But I never liked my name so much as when I finally heard you say it.

How strange to think, were it not for your grandmother's interfering, I might never have had the courage to propose. It was unwelcome at the time, but perhaps God used her to nudge me. Perhaps even to show me how much I really wanted to marry you. And how strange to think, were it not for your mother forbidding us to contact each other, you might never have determined to write to me anyway, accepting my proposal. Both of these godly women worked against us – your mother trying to forbid our love, your grandmother trying to push us together before our time, and both their interference equally unwelcome – and yet God worked for us through them.

When I'm in the very worst circumstances, when there is no food, no sleep, when the worst sort of guard is mocking and threatening me, then I think of those little 'warnings' you gave me about how young and silly you can be. That's when I imagine you rambling around your garden all night with the dog, or putting on a ballgown for no reason, or dragging, all by yourself, a Christmas tree to my prison.

You thought these warnings would be enough to keep me from marrying you. On the contrary, they became one major reason why I did want to. Did you think I couldn't be silly too? Perhaps I don't get the chance often, but how I shall love being silly with you and our children. We will forget these years of separation. Like your mother and grandmother's meddling, they will be something that should have worked against us but will really work for us. The separation will bring us closer.

To be quite honest, I've sometimes been afraid you might have said yes out of pity. I now know it wasn't that, and that you felt as I did. We knew we belong together, and today we know it more than ever.[1]

You couldn't understand why I wanted you. Dear Maria, every man wants a woman who is young and brilliant and beautiful. The wonder of it was that you should ever have considered me. But then, I was 'Dr Bonhoeffer' – and maybe it's also natural that a young woman should want a man with something of a name and a reputation, a man with a future.

That future is still before me, every day. I no longer have your letters, but I think all the time of our wedding, every aspect of it as you described it to me, your every little plan that will one day come to fruition. I can picture our home with all the furniture you've picked out. I can see your face framed by a white veil. Our wedding will be missing some guests, dear ones that the war has taken from us, but we will build a new family, whilst never forgetting those we've lost. We'll name two boys after your father and your brother who have died in this war, and one after my brother who died in the Great War. And perhaps we'll name girls after your mother and grandmother – to show them we've truly forgiven them!

It's midnight now, Saturday. I can sleep now …

With all my dearest love,

Dietrich

---

1. This paragraph is a direct quote. As a political prisoner Dietrich was allowed to send letters to his family and fiancée (although these were strictly supervised) and this fictional letter discusses several things that are mentioned in their real letters, such as wedding details and Maria's relatives interfering in their relationship.

ᔔ TAKING A STAND ᔒ

For the first time in months or years, the prisoners woke up too comfortable to move. The thick feather duvets felt like hugs in a place where no one ever hugged. And as there would apparently be no breakfast, there seemed little motivation to get up.

Dietrich rolled over and thought, as he did every morning, of the phrase Maria had once written him, which he had now adopted: Every morning I think, maybe today is the day! Maybe it was. Maybe this was the day he would be released. Or the day Hitler would be killed. Or the day the war would end. That day had to come someday ... it was like Advent in his childhood, the suspenseful waiting for something that would finally come. A deliverance. Maybe this was even the greatest day in all history, the day Jesus would return.

He checked his watch. It was only a few minutes before six. At six Maria would be doing just what he was doing, studying today's Bible readings and praying. Praying for him. He wondered where she was now: still staying with his parents in Berlin, or with her grandmother Ruth in Bavaria, or with her mother in Pomerania, or with one of the many relatives and friends and hospitals that she helped. He liked to think of her with his parents. He could picture the house so exactly: the furniture, his mother's cheerful 'Good morning', the food on the breakfast table, his room where Maria sat at his own desk to write him – letters he hadn't received for months. She would be so terribly frightened now that he had disappeared. But maybe today would be the day.

By the time Dietrich finished his reading and prayers, the Wolf was already barking threats at the commandant. 'But this is unacceptable! We have had nothing but a couple of small potatoes for three days.'

The commandant was blushing like a boy in the headmaster's office. 'Herr Wolf' –

'You may call me Captain Best.'

'–I have nothing but my apologies to give you. My men, and indeed I, go hungry this morning. There is a possibility we may have access to a motorcycle later to get to a town and bring back food.'

'Food for twenty on a motorcycle?' the Wolf asked bitterly. 'You may bring back enough for your men, but nothing for us.'

'I assure you, it's only a matter of time before we can make arrangements. Please be patient.'

'It is only a matter of time before we faint away – or worse!'

The commandant looked pretty faint himself. 'We are all in the same boat, Captain. The truth is, you yourself are better supplied than most of my men. As political prisoners you are entitled to keep many personal possessions; as soldiers, my men have little but their uniforms.'

'It's hard to feel sorry for the soldiers, Herr Commandant, so long as they still have their guns.' The Wolf sighed. 'Look, perhaps you can at least send up some hot water so we can pretend it's coffee.'

'Yes, Captain Best.'

He said it in the same tone in which he might have said, 'Yes, sir.' The commandant backed out of the door and closed it quietly behind him.

When the Wolf turned around, his face was grim and tired but not angry. 'I have some dried peppermint,' he announced. 'Peppermint tea won't be much comfort for empty stomachs, but at least it's something to go in empty mouths. In the meantime' – he held up an electric razor – 'I notice there are electric sockets here. Any man who wishes a shave is most welcome.'

Dietrich burst out laughing. 'Trust the Wolf to have an electric razor! We may be starved, but at least we can look civilised.' He added in English: 'All dressed up but nowhere to go.'

The Wolf, smiling, bent down to plug in the razor. 'Do you speak English, Bonhoeffer? You might have told me before.'

'Not as good as I would wish. I can make myself understood, but it does not come easily to me to think in English.'

'I know you've spent time in America, but have you ever been in Britain?'

'Oh, yes. There have been a number of times when I've felt somewhat unwelcome in Germany.'

1933

Dietrich loved St Nicholas' Church, one of the oldest buildings in Berlin. Many great men had ministered there, including his favourite hymnwriter, Paul Gerhardt, and now he was getting to see a new pastor inducted: his close friend Franz. They loved to argue and debate almost everything, but they agreed line for line on how terrible the Nazi party was, and particularly on the way they were trying to force the German Church to adopt Nazi policies. The most obvious of these was the Aryan Paragraph, which stated that no person of Jewish blood could be a minister in a Christian church.

Franz was a Jew.

After the service, Dietrich shook hands warmly with his friend. 'I'm sure you'll do a fine job, Franz,' he said. 'Just be sure and come to me if anyone ever asks you a hard question about the Bible. I'll help you out!'

'You'll send them back to me grateful that I'm their minister, not you,' Franz retorted.

'Are you suggesting that I complicate biblical matters?'

'No, you're just very good at telling people what they don't want to hear!'

'I'd like to tell Herr Hitler a few things he doesn't want to hear,' Dietrich muttered.

They were joined by Pastor Niemoller, an older man who ministered to a large, poor church in the city.

'So, Franz, you've made it into the ministry of the German Church – and what a congregation!' he said. 'I only hope you get to stay in it.'

'The Nazis are trying to make the German people think they don't want Jewish ministers,' Franz said.

'Luckily for me, the German people don't seem to agree.'

'And this is the best way to fight them,' Niemoller nodded, 'by showing them the lack of support for their ideas. Make them look ridiculous. Carry on as normal. Provoke them to anger.'

'Pastor, I disagree. There's something to be said for provoking the Nazis to anger, but the time has come for more important action,' Dietrich said. 'Tomorrow the so-called "German Christians" are holding a rally at Berlin University. They're going to nominate Muller as the new Reich Bishop, and if that chucklehead gets in – and he will, if Hitler is as powerful as he thinks – the church will be under serious attack, with no one to defend it against this government.'

'It would be the end of openly teaching the true gospel in Germany,' Niemoller agreed. 'Just think of Muller's greatest ideas – from "the love of the German people hates everything weak" to "the idea of grace is un-German".'

'What are you going to do at this meeting? Are you speaking?' Franz asked Dietrich.

'Yes – with my feet. When they nominate Muller, my students and I are going to walk out. And we could certainly use you two to walk with us. Especially Martin Niemoller! No offence, Franz, but no one knows who you are.'

'Yet,' Franz replied.

The meeting at the university went much as they had all expected. There were a number of Nazi officers in attendance alongside the ministers and theology students. The pro-Nazis spoke the loudest, shouting and waving their arms in an imitation of Hitler's own speaking style, but when Dietrich and his students stood to walk out in protest, almost all the students in the hall went with them. Suddenly it was the protesters who had most of the audience!

They marched outside and gathered around a statue of the philosopher Hegel. Dietrich was excited. 'This is just like what happened in Scotland in 1843,' he said. 'Part of the Church of Scotland felt that the government was interfering too much in the church's affairs, and they walked out of their General Assembly and formed the Free Church. This could be a new beginning for us – for the whole church in Germany!'

His friend Karl Barth, the most important Christian teacher in Germany, overheard. 'Bonhoeffer, do you hear what you're saying? We can't just tear apart the whole national church just like that, without thinking about it. It has to be an absolute last resort – so it's really obvious that we're the true church, and they're the ones who have departed from us.'

'What could be more of a departure from Scripture than demanding that only white, non-Jewish people can belong to the church?' Dietrich demanded. 'How can we possibly call ourselves a national church if we can't be a church for all Germany's people?'

'We've been thinking,' Franz said, 'this may be a chance to make a stand for the truth. We could convene a Council, just as the early church did when there was an argument about the meaning of Scripture. The ministers of all Europe's churches could get together to debate how Christ really wants us to live. We couldn't lose that argument – the Nazi policies are just too brutal. It's a way to defeat their ridiculous ideas hands-down.'

'And if they don't listen to that,' Bonhoeffer added eagerly, 'the church will go on strike! No weddings, no funerals, no baptisms, no services. The conservative church-goers will be furious. There would be chaos – imagine the disruption of cancelled marriage ceremonies, funerals with no one to bury the dead. Thousands turning up to church on Sunday morning and finding the doors locked. We could spark a revolution from the pew! That'll force the Nazis to give in and stop interfering with us.'

'You two young chaps have let your imaginations run away with you,' Niemoller said. 'We must wait and see how this "Aryan Paragraph" turns out – we haven't tried every option for stopping it yet. These Nazi thugs might do their best to meddle in church affairs, but I'm quite sure that Hitler himself is a reasonable man. There must be a misunderstanding somewhere – he'll set it right. I've requested an audience with him.'

'Have you gone blind?' Dietrich said, horrified. 'Look at everything he's done since he came to power, everything he did to get power. Adolf Hitler serves no one but himself. And he will not be satisfied until there is no one left in Germany who disagrees with him and his anti-Christian policies.'

'He's been good for the country,' Niemoller argued. 'Our economy, our national pride.'

'Yes!' cried a student, overhearing. 'We are only against the government interfering in church affairs – we are not against our government!'

'Nor our Fuhrer!' another called, saluting his arm high in the air. 'We are churchmen, but we are patriots too. Heil Hitler!'

And as Dietrich and Franz watched, horrified, all of the students who had walked out with them gave the Nazi salute.

'As if Germany was Hitler!' Franz gasped.

'They're all blind,' Dietrich said grimly. 'But they won't be forever.'

1945

'So it was not a new beginning for the church that day,' said the Wolf.

'No, but as I predicted, Hitler couldn't fool these godly men for long. Once the Aryan Paragraph was in force, the Jewish pastors had to leave their churches, and the other ministers protested against the decision. They formed the Confessing Church, which held to the teachings of the Bible even when the Nazis declared that the Old Testament was too Jewish and had to be thrown out, and that the Cross of Christ showed weakness and therefore that had to go too.

'Karl Barth, our greatest theologian, had to return to Switzerland and safety. My friend Franz Hildebrand left the country to escape the Jewish persecution. Martin Niemoller got his audience with Hitler, saw first-hand what a madman he was, and was soon arrested for his anti-Nazi activities. He's been in jail for eight years now. I saw him in prison a few months ago – he regrets not understanding sooner the evil around him. He's even written a poem about it:

First they came for the Socialists, and I did not speak out –
because I was not a Socialist.

Then they came for the Trade Unionists,
and I did not speak out – because I was not a Trade
Unionist.
Then they came for the Jews, and I did not speak out –
because I was not a Jew.
Then they came for me –
and there was no one left to speak for me.'

'And what did you do?' the Wolf asked. 'You saw the truth before anyone else, so you must have been very important in the Confessing Church.'

'As important as I could be,' Dietrich said, 'without being in the country.'

'But where were you?'

Dietrich gave him a wistful smile. 'Your country. I went and pastored two German congregations in London.'

'I hate to say this, but didn't that rather smack of running away?'

'Oh, that's what Barth said – and he was my mentor, so it hurt a little bit. But he didn't see yet that German pastors were going to need allies. Being in London allowed me to make contacts with important people and tell them what kind of struggle the German Church was facing. I was invited to Lambeth Palace, where the Archbishop of Canterbury promised to support the Confessing Church and publicly criticise the "German Christians." It was also there that I met a good friend who would be our greatest champion in trying to get the British government to work with the Resistance. The Bishop of Chichester' –

' – George Bell,' the Wolf finished, his thin, tight face splitting into a big smile. 'It seems we have a mutual friend, Bonhoeffer!'

'A kinder and more thoughtful man I never met,' Dietrich replied. 'And one whom I have no doubt is still fighting for us.'

A PROTESTANT MONASTERY

As Dietrich and the Wolf talked about their old friend Bishop Bell, they were distracted from their conversation by the sound of another prisoner muttering to himself. The Wolf looked around the room, then drained his tea and laughed quietly into his cup.

'If you have a joke, please share it,' Dietrich said. 'Like everything else, they're in short supply these days.'

'That little fellow is the joke,' the Wolf grinned, nodding across the room at a short man sitting bolt upright on his bed, talking to himself all alone on the other side of the room. 'I've never met someone so "yellow" in all my life! See what Rascher wrote for his name.'

'The Coward.'

'His brother was a brave man – he had a hand in the Stauffenberg plot to kill Hitler last year. He was executed, and this poor fellow was arrested just for being family. Thinks it's the guards coming for him whenever the door opens. Every time he hears me barking at the commandant his legs turn to water.'

Dietrich smiled thinly. 'Barking – is that why they call you Herr Wolf?'

'Oh, that's just my code name from the Nazis. My actual name is Best. Though clearly I'm not, or I wouldn't be here.'

'I heard someone say you were a spy?'

'Yes, one of Britain's finest, or so I thought. I was trying to make contact with the German Resistance at the start of the war, but someone set me up and I was captured. I've been camped out in one prison or another for the whole of the war. Six years nearly. It's all right – they gave me all my possessions, and the guards aren't so bad once you learn to handle them. But men like that Coward, they bring down the spirits of everyone around them. Fear is contagious; that's why it's so offensive in a place like this.'

'He must be suffering greatly from so much fear,' Dietrich reflected. 'You'd help him more by talking to him, not about him. We must strengthen one another. After all, we have precious little here besides each other. We're like our own little village – or monastery.'

'What does a Lutheran pastor know about life in a monastery?' the Wolf grinned.

'Dear fellow, I practically ran one!'

1935

The man was still a long distance away, but already it was clear he was headed straight for Dietrich. Dietrich was walking along the beach, where he'd been playing games with the seminary students, and it looked as if he and the other young man were going to meet halfway.

The stranger was thin, dark, and dressed like someone from a small town – decent but not fashionable. 'I'm looking for the seminary director,' he said. 'The other students seemed to think you were the man to ask. I just got here today.'

'Dietrich Bonhoeffer,' he replied, holding out his hand.

It took the man a moment to respond. 'You – you are the director of the seminary?'

'Yes, but you may call me Brother Bonhoeffer.'

'I'm sorry. I mistook you for just another student!'

'Yes, the others made that mistake when they came too. I may be young, but I have some ideas. And you are Brother …'

'Bethge. Eberhard Bethge.'

'Come and walk back to the seminary with me. I'll tell you the rules.'

'The rules?'

'We have some radical ideas here, Brother Bethge. For example, everyone must choose a confessor, and talk to that person about the sins and temptations we're struggling with. The Bible says we should be accountable to one another.'

'I can see this is going to be a challenging year,' Eberhard said, laughing.

'But there's one rule even more important.' Dietrich stopped and looked at his new pupil very seriously. 'No one is ever to speak a word about another student if he isn't present. It's cowardly to criticise someone behind his back, and gossip won't be tolerated.'

'That sounds pretty sensible to me.'

'It solves problems before they ever happen, but it's more difficult than you imagine. Oh, and there's one thing we do believe in here that's not exactly spelled out in the Apostles' Creed.'

Eberhard stiffened. 'What's that?'

'Having fun. And we're missing out on today's football game!' Dietrich clapped him on the back and ran down to the pitch, where the other students were already in the middle of a match.

That night the students and staff met together for dinner in the big hall. It was so exciting to look around all their young faces and know not only that these were men who wanted to serve Jesus, but that they truly loved Him – and would not allow any government to tell them what to believe or who could be in their church. All these humble, Christlike men …

'Excuse me, Herr Director,' whispered one of the kitchen staff, bending low beside his chair. 'The kitchen is overflowing and we haven't got a full staff yet – would it be possible to ask if one or two of the students would help with the dishes?'

Bonhoeffer stood up. 'Brothers, I hope you all enjoyed your dinner. The cook has asked if anyone will volunteer to help with the dishes.'

The men barely registered this request. They all expected someone else to volunteer. Minutes passed and no one even noticed that the Director hadn't sat back down. But then someone said, 'Where's Brother Bonhoeffer?'

The men exchanged a guilty look, and then they all rose at the same moment and trooped down to the kitchen. 'Oh, he can't be!' someone groaned.

But he was – the Director was washing the dishes, and chatting away to the kitchen porter as if the boy were a fellow professor. When he heard the door handle rattle, he looked round, shot his students one look through the window, then turned back to what he was doing. He had locked the door so that they couldn't come and help.

The students slunk away, down to the beach, where they waited for the Director to show up and deliver a pointed lecture on Christ's servanthood. But when he got to the beach, Brother Bonhoeffer never said a word about dishes. Instead he told stories about his year in New York and invited the students back to the rec room to listen to his recordings of black gospel music.

As the term went on, Bonhoeffer chose someone to confess his sins to – he insisted on being bound by all the same rules as the students. And he chose Eberhard Bethge. The first time they met in the Director's study, face-to-face as equals, Eberhard could hardly keep from blushing.

'I suppose the first thing I should confess is curiosity,' he said. 'I can't imagine what terrible transgressions you have committed, Dietrich. And perhaps I shouldn't want to know what kind of sin you commit – but I do.'

'That's part of the reason we do this, to show that we are all human after all. Would you like to hear about my temper first, and my impatient way with people? Or the terrible depression that comes over me from time to time? Or my spiritual pride that I am a seminary director at such a young age? There are many other things I could choose too. You'll see so much more if you know me long enough.'

Eberhard leaned forward. 'All right, so these are some of the things you struggle with. But what am I supposed to tell you about them? It's not as if we prescribe penance in this seminary.'

'The most important thing is not to tell me it's all right, or that those are just little sins, or that they're understandable. It's not for you to judge me, but neither is it for you to forgive me – remember that only Jesus can forgive. I'll show you what I mean. You tell me about one of your own sins.'

Eberhard winced. 'As a matter of fact, I broke your rule. I spoke to another student about someone who wasn't there. Someone I don't like particularly. I said that I thought he had no creative or interesting thoughts.'

Dietrich nodded. 'Did the one you were speaking to also dislike this fellow?'

'I don't think he had any particular feelings toward him.'

'And do you think he likes the chap more or less, now that he's heard your opinion?'

'I suppose less.'

'So you have poisoned one brother against another.'

Eberhard flushed. 'You're supposed to make me feel worse?'

'I'm supposed to help you see sin as God sees it. Only then will we be motivated to repent. Eberhard, it's easy for seminary students to feel good about themselves. They can feel that they know God pretty well, that they're even giving their careers to God. Perhaps they think that God therefore owes them something. This is to remind us that we are all, like Paul, the worst of sinners in God's eyes.'

'It's humiliating!'

'Yes, it is, until you understand that I don't think any less of you because of what you did.'

'How can that be?'

'Because I've broken that rule too. Everyone has. But generally only once – that's all it takes to see the damage it can do.'

'Should I confess to the fellow that I gossiped about him?'

'No, that's another important rule. Telling him would ease your conscience, but it would make him feel worse. Here we are learning to put our brothers before ourselves.'

'Dietrich, I'm not sure how I'm going to survive confession time every week.'

Dietrich laughed. 'I'll tell you more about my own sin, and you'll feel better in a moment.'

1945

'If you don't mind me saying so,' the Wolf told him, 'your seminary sounds terrifying.'

Dietrich laughed. 'It was a place of growth. Growth is rarely comfortable.'

'I sense in your story a form of rebuke for the way I spoke about the poor Coward.'

'I disapprove of this whole business of distilling a person down to one trait. That fellow is more than a coward. Just as I am more than the pastor who plotted to kill Hitler.'

'You're also the pastor who washed the dishes,' the Wolf said.

Dietrich smiled. 'Let's say I'm the pastor who's willing to take responsibility for whatever needs done – the things no one else wants to dirty their hands on.'

'In my book, Pastor, that takes exceptional bravery.'

'This is a room of exceptionally brave men and women,' Dietrich replied. 'All except one – one ordinary man who expresses the fear we all feel. Let's not punish him for it.'

༄ FEAR ༄

By the time Dietrich finished his story, the Coward was
no longer talking to himself. He was trying to read a
book he'd borrowed from another prisoner, but his eyes
darted restlessly across the words and he never seemed
to turn a page. Dietrich went over to him and asked if
he could sit on the bed.

'Sir,' he said, 'I think the name Rascher has given you
is most unfair. It's not surprising a man in prison would
feel anxious – there's no need to make fun of someone
for it.'

'Well, quite! Naturally my life is of value to me, and
I don't relish losing it – I don't see why that should make
me a laughing stock! Just because my brother was stupid
enough to plot against the Fuhrer, why should I be in
prison expecting a bullet in my back every day?'

'I can see that you're troubled all the time.'

'How is it that the rest of you aren't? I'm stalked by
death. I see it all around me; I feel it waiting for me day
by day. I can't stop hearing the shots and screams that
I heard all the time in the camp where they kept me
before. And what isn't death, in these days, is misery

and cold and hunger. Naturally one hates all the violence and corruption of this Nazi regime, but why take a stand when one can't possibly hope to make a difference? Well, I hope my dear General brother thought it was all worth it – all his plots and scheming – when they shot him.'

A tremor went through the little man and tears rose to his eyes. It was as if he saw his brother again, not as a dead General, but as the little boy who had grown up alongside him.

'That's the worst thing we can suffer,' Dietrich said wearily. 'Not what they do to us, but what they do to our families and friends.'

'All due respect, Pastor, but you took a stand against the Nazi policies from the beginning. I know that much. You put yourself here.'

Dietrich nodded. 'Yes, I did, but I could do nothing else. A church that would agree to expelling all the Jews was no Christian church. A church that denied the whole Old Testament because of its Jewishness, a church that denied the cross of Christ – that is a church of the devil.'

'So you say, but perhaps some men, some good men, would find a way to justify remaining in it.'

'Many good men did. Many said they needed to fight the corruption from within. Many said they needed to care for their families and their congregations. Many said they could put up with these doctrines without agreeing with them. And I don't blame them.'

'Really?' the Coward asked, blinking. 'You call it a devilish church and yet you don't blame those who stayed in it?'

'I can't condemn a man for choosing to live rather than die. Everyone must make that decision for himself, and answer for it too.' Dietrich bowed his head. 'Besides, it took me some time to find the right path.'

1933

'Dietrich,' Sabine said, 'Thank you for coming so quickly.' Her black mourning dress matched her dark hair and the sleepless shadows under her eyes. It was hard to see her this way: his twin, the only friend he'd had since before he was born, and still the person who knew him best in the world.

Dietrich hugged her, his hat in his hand. 'Of course I come when my sister needs me. I'm so sorry about your father-in-law.'

'He was a good man. Come, Gert is expecting you.'

He went with her into the study, where her husband Gert, also in black, was just hanging up the phone. Everything was in a bustle throughout the house, preparations for the funeral speeding along.

'Ah, you've come,' Gert said, standing and holding out his hand. 'I know you're busy.'

'Never too busy for you. I wish I could be of some comfort. It has been a hard year with Jews being expelled from university jobs too.'

'And losing my father is worse than losing my job. I can always go to a new country where Jews are still allowed to teach, but I shall never see my father on earth again.' He bowed his head. 'I know he was never baptised, but my father believed Jesus was the Messiah. He was a Christian even if he never professed it publicly. Dietrich, we want you to preach at his funeral.'

Dietrich fiddled with his hat brim. 'Why, Gert, I don't know what to say.'

'Just preach about any verses you want.'

'I mean, I don't know what to say to you now. The Nazis will certainly take notice of a Christian preacher conducting a funeral for an unbaptised Jew.'

'Dietrich!' Sabine said. 'You've been outspoken about your belief that Jews should be included in the life of the church.'

He sighed. 'That's why I might get in so much trouble. Bishop Muller[1] and his gang are looking for any excuse to remove me from the ministry. Or worse. If I preach for the funeral of a Jew, they'll have one.'

'You mean if you practise what you preach' –

Gert held up his hand. 'Sabine, please. We won't argue over Father's funeral. Dietrich, these are troubled times, and I don't blame you.'

'It's just that I can't continue my work with the church or my fight against the government if I'm arrested for some small offence like that.'

Gert shook his head. 'You don't need to explain. I understand perfectly. And we would never wish you to undergo the kind of persecution we've experienced. Your work must go on.'

Dietrich stood up and took his hat. 'Gert, Sabine, a year ago I would have preached without a second thought. I want nothing more than to do this for you.'

---

1. Muller was the Nazis' choice to oversee the whole of the German national Church. He was a coarse man of openly sinful habits, and all too ready to give up Bible truths and teach whatever lies the Nazis wanted. Every powerful person in the church knew that Dietrich was making a stand against the Nazis influencing the church, and wanted to shut down his ministry.

'You are doing what you must,' Gert said, 'and no doubt that is the right decision. Forgive me, brother, but I have much to arrange for the burial.'

Sabine walked him out of the study, both of them silent. At the door Dietrich looked up at her. He had trouble meeting her eye. 'Sabine, I have added to your burdens.'

'Gert is right, there is nothing to forgive. If anyone is to blame for this burden, it's Hitler, not you, Dietrich.'

He pressed her hand. 'I'm very sorry for your loss,' he said softly, and left.

1945

'That's not such a very great confession,' the Coward said. 'I daresay it was the right decision – certainly the wisest.'

'So my supervisor assured me. But you see, it was a betrayal of my sister, of my beliefs, and of my faith – I should have cast myself upon God's protection, knowing He doesn't desert those who show integrity. In the months afterward I was in no doubt that I had done the wrong thing. I'd been blinded by fear, and I could barely understand my own frame of mind. Sabine and Gert never said another word about the matter.'

'Still, if that's the most you've ever betrayed your own convictions, you're doing better than most in this moral chaos we find ourselves in.'

'There was another time,' Dietrich said.

1939

The Empire State Building and the Chrysler Building stuck up like two teeth from the jagged New York skyline.

They were finished now: the world's tallest buildings in first and second place. This time, as the ship sailed past the Statue of Liberty, the mood on board was not one of delight, but of relief. Many of the European passengers were not merely travelling – they were escaping.

And in the city, there was no clatter and mess of construction. Instead, many of the workers who had built those skyscrapers stood in long queues at soup kitchens and unemployment offices. The stock market had taken hold of the country, leaving families with no savings and no jobs.

However, while there was no money to add more monsters to the skyline, there was money to allow Dietrich to do what he did best. The word had gone out among his friends – 'Dietrich must come to America, or he'll be drafted to fight for the Nazis' – and they had found him work lecturing at Union Seminary and ministering to German refugees.

Dietrich was happy to see his old friends in New York, but everywhere he went, no matter what he did, he could think of nothing but Germany. What was happening there? Were his family and friends all right? What were the Nazis up to? Had they closed his seminary? Very little news was leaking out from Hitler's Germany. The safety of America felt like a prison when he was so cut off from those he loved. For the first time he felt really homesick, not just for sauerkraut and knodels,[2] or even family, but for German language and humour and scenery. He longed for the very air of Berlin. It had never felt so far away before.

---

2. Knodels are large, thick dumplings usually served in soup.

He read every European newspaper he could find, and even went to cinemas that showed nothing but newsreels, but the Nazi government carefully controlled information, and he could learn nothing new. So in New York, waiting on letters that could take weeks to arrive, Dietrich feared the worst.

And the more he wondered what was happening at home, the more he wondered what he was doing in America.

He might be safe from the Nazis, but he had no peace. The skyscrapers closed in on him like a cage. It had seemed like a smart decision to come here, but it was not where God wanted him. He felt like Jonah running away from Nineveh, with the sea waves crashing down and the storm roaring around him.

Dietrich knew he couldn't keep running. He was called to go and suffer with his people and one day, Lord willing, to help rebuild the country. He knew he would be drafted, and he was determined not to fight for the Nazis – and he also knew he would be arrested if he refused. He couldn't see any future except for hiding, prison or execution. But he knew God had a plan.

Only three weeks after arriving in New York, Dietrich decided to get the next passenger ship back to Germany. He was just in time – it was the last one before the raging war shut down the Atlantic.

1945

'Well, bravo,' the Coward said sourly. 'I see how well God protected you.'

'When Christ calls a man, He invites him to come and die,' Dietrich replied. 'My life is His. As the apostle Paul said, I am crucified with Christ.[3] And like Paul, I can even praise God from prison.'

'I grew up in church, you know. I was baptised and confirmed like anyone else. How come I don't feel like singing in my jail cell?'

'You know, we spend all our lives fearing death. But we understand so little about it. How do we know it's not the most glorious and wonderful experience of our lives?[4] You see, if we really know Jesus, we can't fear going to be with Him. And nobody really comes to Jesus without longing to go and be with Him – it's a kind of homesickness, just as real as I felt in New York.'

'I'll take your word for it.'

And then Dietrich was sad, for he was offering true peace and freedom, and the Coward had turned away.

---

3. Galatians 2:20: I have been crucified with Christ and I no longer live, but Christ lives in me. The life I now live in the body, I live by faith in the Son of God, who loved me and gave himself for me (NIV 2011 edition).

4. Dietrich really said this, as well as that nobody really comes to Christ without longing to go and be with Him from that time on. What comforting thoughts when we are scared of death!

✎ A MUSICAL EVENING ✎

After their sparse breakfast of herbal tea, the Matron did her best to impose order. While the men discussed politics and the progress of the war, she started to collect any laundry that they could spare. The housekeeper provided a tub of hot water and a little soap, and the Matron pressed the Blonde Bombshell into service too. It was she who came to Dietrich's bed to collect his things.

Short, stout, and businesslike, the Blonde was not much of a bombshell at all – though that might have come as news to her. She loved movies, and had clearly studied every gesture and expression of Marlene Dietrich, the greatest German movie star, putting on her best impersonation of the actress every time she spoke to a man. She always had her blouse buttoned a bit too low or her skirt rolled a bit too high, and none of the male prisoners were ever quite sure where to look. Dietrich did what he always did: he tried to focus on her eyes, and see what it was that she needed deep down.

'Hey, Pastor, what've you got for washing?' she asked.

'I only wish I had something to wash! I'm wearing my entire wardrobe.'

That button looks kind of loose,' she said, touching his arm.

'Oh no, it'll hold,' he said hurriedly. 'Anyway, I haven't got anything else to put on, so I can't take it off.'

'You don't have to, you just hold your arm still. I can sew a sleeve button with my eyes closed.'

'Please don't try!'

'All right. But I am going to sew the button. I insist.'

'You're really being too kind, Fraulein.'

'Aw, if I don't do this, that Matron will make me do some real work. I'd rather have an excuse to sit and talk to you.'

'Very well, if I can be of service,' Dietrich said, resigned. 'Were you a seamstress before you ended up here?'

'Nah. I can do a bit of everything, though. Useful in my line of work.'

'Which is?'

She shot him a mysterious look, one eyebrow raised, and said nothing.

'Come, you can tell me,' Dietrich said. 'What have you got to lose? You're already in prison.'

She leaned in. 'There are spies everywhere. You think these are all real prisoners? I don't. At least one of them is reporting back to the guards on everything we say.'

'Nonsense!'

'That doctor, what's he doing here if he's so involved with the highest government officials? And that posh general who wears his medal day and night – he's no ordinary prisoner.'

Dietrich sighed. 'You don't have to tell me if you don't want to.'

'Let's just say I was meant to be working for the Secret Service, but I had a bit too much to do with their folk.' She nodded violently toward the two English prisoners, who were chatting innocently.

'Ah, a double agent? You were spying for the English when you were meant to be spying for the Nazis.'

'I didn't say that.' She gave him a cryptic smile.

'I fully understand,' Dietrich said dryly. 'Well, we'll be liberated any day now. If you can't tell me what you did before, perhaps you can tell me how you plan to occupy yourself once we're free?'

She got a dreamy look in her eye. 'Oh, I don't know! I was just a girl before the war – I hardly remember it. A drab little life with a drab little family. Life may not be all that safe now, but at least it's exciting. The war was one big adventure for me, I can tell you that much.'

'Rather too adventurous for me,' he replied with a smile. 'All I want to do is settle down in the countryside and go back to writing books that will only be read by a few hundred academics and raise a drab little family of my own.'

'Really? That's the kind of life you actually want?'

'This war has given me enough drama to last a lifetime.'

1939

It was one of the Bonhoeffer family's splendid musical gatherings. Although regular occurrences, they were always treated as festive occasions. The best china was set out for a magnificent tea. All the candles were burning brightly. Bubbles fizzed in cut-crystal goblets and the violinist licked sachertorte[1] crumbs off her fingers as she stood up to take her place. The family headed back to their seats to listen to the next selection, jokes and laughter still pinging through the room. Hans von Dohnanyi, in town for once and free for the family gathering, lightly nudged Dietrich's elbow. 'How often do I get to see you now? Come, sit with your favourite brother-in-law.'

Dietrich had a front seat for the musical performances, but there was something urgent in Hans' voice, and he followed his sister Christel's husband to the back of the room.

When the music started, Hans leaned close to Dietrich and said softly, 'I hear you have a problem. Your conscience does not allow you to fight – but pacifists[2] can be executed for treason. What will you do?'

'I don't know,' Dietrich replied. 'I've been praying God will provide an answer. I'm just trying to carry on with whatever church work I can until the government comes looking for me.'

'God has answered your prayers,' Hans replied. 'He has sent you the Abwehr.'

Dietrich looked at him in amazement. 'Our military intelligence agency is going to solve my problem?'

'Yes. Because we're going to hire you before the army does.'

'Me? A spy?'

---

1. A thick chocolate cake popular in Germany, covered with more chocolate!

2. Pacifists are people who believe that all war is wrong. This attitude was considered weak, criminal, and most un-German and was almost unheard of in Nazi Germany. Dietrich had become a pacifist during his first time in New York, through discussions with a French friend.

'Dietrich.' Hans stood up and gestured for Dietrich to follow him. They went into the empty study where Karl Bonhoeffer normally saw psychiatric patients.

'Now then,' Hans said, leaning against his father-in-law's desk. 'Dietrich, you know that I'm in the Abwehr. Do you think I'm really a spy for the Nazis?'

'I know that you are an honorable man, Hans, and whatever your position or your actions, it's not my place to question them.'

'I work for Wilhelm Canaris – the head of the whole organisation. And do you know the most important thing I do for him? I keep records of every terrible thing the Nazis are doing. So that one day, when all this is over, there will be proof. I even help Jews get out of Germany. Brother, all this runs deeper than you can imagine. You know Hitler is an oaf, but the brutalities that are actually happening – you have no idea. Canaris and I are effectually spying on Hitler, not for him.'

'And that's what you're asking me to be part of?' Dietrich asked slowly.

Hans held up his hands. 'It's a solution to your immediate problem. We could claim that your international church contacts would be useful to the government, and get you hired that way. You wouldn't be drafted by the army. But you might be joining something far more dangerous. You should take some time to think about it.'

'Would it give me freedom to travel?'

'You have to understand, you wouldn't be working for us in name only. You'd be a double agent. Carrying messages to your church contacts all right, but for the Resistance, not the Nazis. If you're caught, or I'm caught, or Canaris – or any number of others – we would all be arrested. And remember the penalty for treason: execution, probably torture too. Consider it all carefully, Dietrich. You might be safer in the army!'

They went back to the recital, but for once Dietrich could not even enjoy his sisters' sweet voices and his favourite composers. When asked to play the piano, he just smiled and said he had a headache – which, by that time, he had. All the rest of the evening he felt as if he was holding his breath. It wasn't every day he made a decision on which his whole life might hang. But then, after all, he had made that decision when he got on the ship in New York. He had known he was coming to Berlin to live or die with his country, and his church.

As everyone put on their coats and hats, well after midnight, Dietrich put his on too. 'I'm going to walk Hans and Christel home,' he told his parents. 'I need the air.'

The streets in their genteel neighbourhood were quiet at that hour. There was no indication that a war was surrounding Germany like a hurricane. Yet Dietrich suddenly felt that war very close.

'You can speak in front of Christel,' Hans said. 'She knows as much as I've told you.'

'I want to join you,' Dietrich said.

'Think carefully, darling,' Christel murmured. 'You are a pastor, not a warrior or a spy. Are you really willing to betray your country, even in a just cause?'

'Christel,' he replied, 'if you see a runaway cart hurtling down a busy street, it's not enough just to bandage the people it runs down. You need to shove a spoke in the wheel to stop it altogether. I've counted the cost, and that's what I want to be. A spoke in the wheel.'[3]

1945

'Oh, we're all spokes here,' the Blonde said. 'Some good we've done. The cart just keeps on roaring down the street, picking up speed. First it ran over people. Then countries. It may yet run over us.'

'Are you afraid of death, like that fellow?' Dietrich asked, nodding toward the Coward.

'Me, afraid?' Her eyes sparkled. 'I came into this war half hoping to die, Pastor. My life wasn't just drab before – actually it was pretty terrible. I don't want to go into it, but …'

'But if you wanted to die, it must have been very bad indeed.'

'And working against governments and nations, facing death at any time – why, I'd never felt more alive. I confess, when I was arrested, I did think I was going to get a bullet that very day, and I wasn't quite so excited about it then. Still, what shall I do when it's all over? I can't face the life I had before.'

'What you need, Fraulein, is a purpose. My purpose, when this is all over, is not just to rebuild my own life and start my own family, but to rebuild the country and the church. I didn't succeed in stopping the evil, but perhaps God will use me to heal the wounds of so many.'

---

3. This is one of Bonhoeffer's most famous quotes, justifying why a person might act against his government.

ETHICS

The morning dragged on. There was no structure to the day as there would have been at a normal prison camp. Boredom set in; the prisoners had almost forgotten how to fill time on their own terms. Dietrich sat and played the Coward at chess on a set owned by, of course, the Wolf.

'Don't you wish the world's problems were as simple as chess?' the Coward asked.

'Chess is not simple – and that's why we like it,' Dietrich replied. 'It's just like the real world: there are infinite possibilities and moves. There's always someone who can outplay you. There are pieces that have great power and movement, and pieces that are very limited – but can still be powerful in the right place.'

'But at least the problems on the board are in black and white. In the real world it is not always so easy to tell right from wrong.'

'I don't think it's so difficult to tell,' Dietrich replied. 'Not these days. Not in Germany.'

'You say that now, but ten years ago Nazism took us by surprise. Nobody but the powerless, angry working men voted for Hitler in the beginning. And even fewer people thought the war was a good idea. But when he started winning, most people liked that. And many felt they had to serve their country in a time of war even if they disagreed with Hitler. Many good men are still fighting. It looks to me like Germany is coloured in shades of grey. If you see in black and white, you are unusual for these times.'

'Yes, there are many individual situations where it's hard to know the right thing to do, but most of us are in this prison because we at some time recognised the Nazis in all their blackness.'

'Do you remember when that moment came for you?'

'I thought they were rotten from the start. But' – Dietrich took off his glasses and rubbed them on a corner of his shirt – 'there was a moment I knew we had to take action, and I had to help.'

1940

A sunny day on the German border, an outdoor café, rather nice coffees and pastries on the table. Dietrich's best friend and former student Eberhard sat in the other chair, squinting into the sunlight. The voices around them chattered in German, while Lithuanians – for this had, until recently, been Lithuania rather than Germany – waited on tables and swept the streets. Shoppers and businessmen started their day with espresso, basking in the warmth. It felt like a dozen trips Dietrich and Eberhard had made before, half work and half holiday, meeting with pastors and preaching at churches.

Suddenly a loudspeaker in front of the café crackled into life. 'Attention,' shouted a deep German voice. 'This is an important announcement for all patriots of the Fatherland. France has surrendered to Germany. Our flag now flies from the Arc de Triomphe!'

By our flag he meant not the German tricolour but the Nazi swastika.

The café erupted into shouts of victory. Those lazy, content breakfasters jumped up on their tables and started screaming out the national anthem, 'Deutschland, Deutschland uber alles': [Germany conquers all]. Eberhard and Dietrich stared at each other in horror. They had assumed the inexperienced Hitler would be a disaster in wartime. After a few lost battles, the war would be over and Hitler would be deposed. They had never dreamed Germany would subdue other countries, would win. The war would go on. The killing would go on. Hitler would go on.

The song finished in cheers. As the Lithuanians looked on in silence – for they knew what it was to be conquered – the Germans stood at attention and shot their arms out in the Nazi salute. 'Heil Hitler! Heil Hitler!'

And then Dietrich stood up. He raised his arm. 'Heil Hitler!'

Eberhard's mouth fell open. Dietrich glanced down and quickly bent to speak to him. 'Are you crazy? Stand up, quickly, or they'll see you! We'll face trouble and prison, but not over this ridiculous salute.'

Eberhard slowly stood and held out his arm. 'Heil Hitler,' he said.

It was not safe to talk on the street. It wasn't until they were back in the hotel that they could speak privately.

'Dietrich, we've always been anti-Nazi, but it's more than that now, isn't it?' Eberhard asked. 'You're in the Resistance.'

Dietrich looked at him steadily. 'Think carefully about the questions you ask. It could be dangerous for you to know the answers.'

Eberhard thought for a moment. 'Have you done anything yet? Anything that could get you arrested?'

Dietrich shrugged. 'I haven't done anything myself that could be traced with evidence. But I work for, and with, people that have. We are all tied up together. I don't want to get you tied into it too.'

'I'm going to be drafted – it's just a matter of time. Look, I hate this war as much as you do. But I do have a reason for wanting to stay out of trouble.'

'What's that?'

Eberhard shrugged, with a nervous smile. 'Your niece.'

Now it was Dietrich's turn to look shocked. 'I thought you were sweet on Renate! But is it serious?'

'I want to marry her. I was going to ask your advice on persuading her parents – what will they think? She's half my age! But … you have more important things on your mind.'

'My dear friend, nothing is more important than happiness surviving this war. That people still have celebrations and weddings to look forward to in all this misery – that's evidence of God's blessing.[1] You have been practically part of the family for years, and now we could really be cousins!'

---

1. A quote from Bonhoeffer. It's wonderful that we can still enjoy God's blessings even when surrounded by suffering!

Although conversation then turned to more pleasant things, it was impossible from that moment ever to forget that Dietrich was in a dangerous position. He still made trips to speak to other theologians and churches, but Eberhard knew he was also making contacts and updating Germany's enemies on the plans of the Resistance. As he'd predicted, he himself was drafted into the army and sent to Italy. Dietrich's courage and convictions continued to stick in his mind, and Eberhard also worked for the Resistance in whatever way he could, even as he fought for Germany. However, he finally managed to persuade Dietrich's sister and brother-in-law, Ursula and Reinhard, that he was a good match for their daughter Renate, and soon he had a fiancée to look out for.

One night he and Dietrich were at a Resistance friend's house, and a young officer they hadn't met before was there.

'Dr Bonhoeffer,' the young man said. He shook hands rather than giving the Hitler salute. 'My name is Werner.'

'How do you do?' Dietrich asked cautiously.

'You're a man of God,' Werner said. He looked pale and he couldn't stop fidgeting with his hands.

'Something is bothering you?' Dietrich asked.

'A theological question.' He took a deep breath and burst out with it. 'If I killed Hitler, would that be wrong? I have access. I'm on the staff of one of the highest Reich military officers – we see the Fuhrer all the time. I have a gun. I could get close. If I pulled the trigger …?'

He couldn't seem to finish the sentence, except with his bright, fearful eyes.

'You are worried about how God will judge you.'

'Yes.'

'Of course I cannot tell you that exactly, though I have thought about it a great deal – how he will judge all of us. To tell the truth, I believe we are all guilty. If we pull the trigger to kill another human being, we are guilty. If we pass by an opportunity to end all this horror by the taking of one life, we are guilty.'

'But then which is worse?'

'In my view the worst thing would be to kill Hitler without any plan for what happens next. Say you pull the trigger. His closest officers immediately take his place, and the violence only gets worse as they avenge his death. If there's a system in place – if good generals and politicians are ready to step in – if the Allied powers have agreed to give us time to restart our government – then it might do some good. But a rash shooting? No better than murder, and perhaps worse, for many would suffer as a consequence.'

'You seem determined not to tell me what I should do,' the young man said helplessly. 'If you could do it, would you kill Hitler?'

'Yes. If it was all in place, if the right people were ready, and I had the chance to do it, I would.'

'Well done, Pastor,' said a new voice, grinning from a corner of the room.

'Ah,' Dietrich said, pointing in its direction. 'Yes, I'm a pastor. That's the thing. I would resign from the church first. I could not let it seem as if they were involved in such a thing.'

'And anyway,' the voice said, 'what chance would a preacher have to kill the Fuhrer? It's not as if Hitler goes to church and you could pull a gun out of the pulpit! Do you even know how to shoot? It's very different to talk about killing a man when you yourself will never have to do it.'

'You're right, I have no opportunity. Nor do I have any great understanding of guns or bombs. All I have is this: I know that I am responsible. I didn't vote for Hitler, but my country did. I haven't persecuted any Jews, but my country does. I am here, and it's the responsibility of all of us who know better to do what we can. Not just talk, but do. So if I got a good chance, and my contacts asked me to take the shot, I would do it. And God help me.'

'That's as good an answer as I could have hoped for,' Werner said. 'What do you think, sir?'

The owner of the voice walked out into the light. He was in an officer's uniform, a tall, handsome man with a patch over one eye. He crossed over to Dietrich, who slowly stood up.

'Do you know who I am?'

'Count von Stauffenberg,' Dietrich said. 'Of course I do.' He hesitated. 'Are you going to report me?'

The Count smiled slightly. 'No, Pastor, I believe I'll take your advice. And thank you for speaking to Werner. You see, I thought it was better if someone other than myself asked these questions.'

'So you are the man with the conscience,' Dietrich said.

The Count took Dietrich's hand and shook it firmly. 'And you are the chaplain to the Resistance.'

1945

The Coward was silent for a moment. Then he said, 'Werner was one of my brother's associates. He was a passionate young man. It's possible you stopped him from doing some rash action' – he held up a pawn – 'shooting down Hitler with no preparation.'

'Stauffenberg would have restrained him if I hadn't,' Dietrich replied. He moved both the white knight and white pawn to challenge the black king. 'There they were, in an ideal situation. The bomb prepared, Hitler's closest advisers in one room where they could all be killed at once, a network of allies set up to take over the government. It looks like check, if not checkmate. And what happens?' He moved a black bishop between the black king and the white knight. 'A table leg gets in the way and absorbs the blast. Hitler gets away with a few scratches and a tattered suit.'

He picked up the black king and used it to knock over the white knight and pawn.

'People say they died bravely – whatever that means,' the Coward said. 'Stauffenberg called out, "Long live free Germany" the instant before the bullets hit him.'

'They knew God, and they are with Him now. But the rest of us …' Dietrich moved the black pieces, one by one, to surround the remaining white pieces. 'Everyone who was ever close to them is dead or in danger. Quite a few men in this room are imprisoned because of Stauffenberg. And it's a privilege, for I firmly believe that only those who resisted Hitler with all their might will be vindicated by history.'[2]

'Looks like checkmate to all of us,' the Coward said, nodding at the board.

---

2. This was something Stauffenberg believed. He knew Hitler's assassination would come too late to stop the war or even get Germany better terms from the Allies, but felt that it was the right thing to do, for the sake of those who in the future would ask why nobody had ever tried to stop Hitler.

Dietrich laughed. 'Don't believe it, friend. There are a great many more chessboards and a great many more white pieces, and those white pieces surround these black ones a great many times over! I think we may yet hope.'

⤳THE SECRET MISSION ⤶

Around and around. That was what prison life felt like:
a constant parade. The men walked around the table,
taking what exercise they could. Keeping fit because one
day – today? – they might be released, and must be ready
just in case.

As the men marched, they passed each other over and
over again, trading smiles and jokes. So many of them
were distinguished soldiers and generals, but now they
marched for hours like boys just starting basic training.

The Ambassador, who was married to the Matron, had
lost so much weight during his long imprisonment that
his trousers kept slipping, and finally the Wolf stepped
out of line and called him aside. 'Ambassador, you know
I got to keep all my possessions. I have an extensive
wardrobe. Let me offer you some new trousers!'

The Wolf had always been a slim man, so his trousers
fitted the Ambassador well. Yet, when he resumed his
march, something still wasn't quite right. The other men
exchanged glances and smiles, but the Ambassador didn't
take the hint. Finally the Wolf pulled him aside again.

'Erm, Ambassador, if you don't mind me saying, you seem to have left certain ... essential buttons undone.'

'I beg your pardon,' the Ambassador said, loudly enough for the whole room to hear. 'I've never done buttons for myself in my life. I leave that to my wife!'[1]

The men roared with laughter and the Wolf threw up his hands. 'Matron!' he called over to the women at the washing tub. 'There's a more important piece of laundry over here that needs your attention!'

The Matron, clucking, herded her husband behind the changing screen, and he emerged again with buttons intact.

Drama over, the Ambassador resumed his march, and his wife collapsed in a chair near Dietrich, who was reading one of the few books he had managed to bring on the journey.

'The little ceremonies of everyday life!' Dietrich said with a smile. 'I'm glad to see your husband keeps up what normality he can.'

'An ambassador must retain some vestiges of dignity – so he says!' the Matron smiled. Her Spanish accent sounded fiery when she was shouting at the guards, which she did nearly as frequently as the Wolf, but now, in friendly conversation, it was soft and almost musical.

---

1. This is one of many unlikely and very funny stories told by the Wolf – real name Payne Best – in his book *The Venlo Incident*. Life as a political prisoner was often surprising, including the fact that these valuable prisoners got to keep quite a few personal possessions. Most were not extensively tortured, though they did undergo long and often confused questioning. The ordinary prisoners in concentration camps had it much worse, though it was certainly far from pleasant for the political prisoners in terms of cold, filth, hunger, loneliness, and threat.

'Oh, quite. You must have seen some interesting people when your husband was representing Germany in Spain.'

'The courts, the parliaments, the servants, the food, the music – oh, I loved it. Until Hitler came along. An ambassador represents his government. How could we represent this evil Third Reich we didn't believe in?'

'What did you do?'

'We went to my parents' house in Madrid and tried to disappear. It turns out the Nazis are good at finding people.'

'So I've discovered. They forbade me from publishing any more books, shut down my seminaries, and closed the borders so I couldn't visit other theologians. Luckily I found a way to hide in plain sight.'

'How's that?'

'Oh, I joined the Abwehr. I was a sort of ambassador myself on behalf of the Resistance.'

'That sounds like dangerous work. Who did you meet with?'

'Other influential churchmen. Including an old friend.'

1942

'Dietrich, how good to see you again,' Bishop Bell said, pressing Dietrich's hand warmly. 'But how is it possible? I hear it's not so easy leaving Germany these days.'

'You heard correctly,' Dietrich replied. 'When I went to see my friend Karl Barth in Switzerland, he was afraid I'd turned Nazi! And technically, I am in Sweden on official business. Government business.'

Bell raised his eyebrows. 'Even you?'

'I said technically. You see, the government is allowing me to carry out my normal church-related activities because they think I'm also acting as their messenger.'

'But?'

'Well, I am carrying messages all right. But not for the Nazis. It turns out half of their intelligence service is working against them! All the same, it's most important that no one in Germany finds out I've seen you.'

'Certainly,' the Bishop said, gesturing toward a chair. 'How can I help?'

'George, I know I can trust you. Even years ago, when I was working in London, you know I was involved in anti-Nazi efforts. Now there is a solid plan to overthrow Hitler. It goes to the very top, his own generals and officers. I can give you a list if it would help you build up support back home. We have a device, a date, a place, a plan for how to take over the government when Hitler is dead. But we need help.'

'Military backing would be out of the question.'

'All we need is assurances from the British government that they would give us time to get our new government sorted. A ceasefire until they see if they can work with us. Then we can negotiate the end of the war. I suspect we'd have to agree to giving up all our weapons, though the others in my organisation aren't so keen on that idea.'

'Realistically, Dietrich, it will be total surrender or nothing. I know Mr Churchill, and whether he's looking at Hitler or, well, you, he's not going to accept anything less. No conditions. No weapons.'

'That's hard to swallow. But this war must end at any cost. Do you know what I pray for, George? The defeat of my country. She is harming herself so terribly that the most patriotic thing I can do is pray we lose.[2] It's a terrible thing to have to pray for.'

'My dear fellow, let me be quite frank with you.' The Bishop took off his glasses and folded them carefully on to the desk. 'This isn't the first time the German Resistance has come to me asking for help with an intervention. And of course I believe in it completely. I believe the German people themselves are best placed to defeat Hitler.'

'But?'

'The British government thinks I'm a laughing stock. A bleeding heart wanting to befriend our enemies at the cost of our soldiers' lives and our own freedom. You see, my friend, you still think that the Allies have declared war on the Nazis. In fact, they have declared war on Germany. All Germans.'

'But – but how can that be? Most Germans don't care for Hitler or his inhuman policies. They hate this war. Why, half the men in Nazi uniform are serving only out of loyalty to the country, not because they believe in his cause.'

'Say one of our Spitfires is shot down by one of your fellows. Does our pilot, falling to the earth, care whether the chap who shot him down is a Nazi or merely "loyal to Germany"?'

Dietrich could barely believe it – that the British and their allies had declared war not just on the cruel and anti-Jewish Nazis, but on all the good people he knew. His family. His friends. Himself. He lowered his head into his hands.

'I'm terribly sorry, Dietrich.'

---

2. Bonhoeffer did admit to this, and it was shocking in a country where nationalism and Christianity were seen as almost the same thing. We must be very careful about confusing loyalty to our nation with loyalty to God.

'We will carry on,' Dietrich murmured. 'We'll overthrow him anyway.'

'I wish above all things that I could be of help,' Bell replied. 'Of course I will try again to speak to my government, but I want you to be prepared for failure. If there's anything I can do personally, you have only to ask.'

Dietrich looked up. 'British Christians and German Christians love the same God. You can ask Him to help us.'

'That I do, every day. And what shall I pray for you yourself, Dietrich?'

He didn't have to think. 'Pray that He will give me the strength to face whatever I shall have to face. Pray that I shall overcome.'

As he arrived back in Berlin a few days later, there was a sense of crackling tension in the city. People murmured in low voices on the buses and craned their necks, staring in every direction. There seemed to be more soldiers on the street, checking papers. There was a group of sunny-faced blond youths standing around, laughing, and as he passed them, Dietrich turned to see what was so funny.

They were laughing at a quite ordinary, prosperous-looking man walking down the street. He was wearing a homburg hat and a well-cut suit and overcoat and shiny shoes. He looked, in fact, considerably richer than the laughing boys. He even carried himself with an air of dignity, refusing to take any notice of them or their jeers.

But there was something different about him, all right. Sewn on to his coat sleeve was a roughly-cut patch in the shape of a star with six points. The Star of David. Dietrich had seen it painted crudely on to shop windows, but never before had he seen it marking a person. A Jew.

As he walked from the bus stop to his parents' house, Dietrich saw that star patch on a few more coats, and each time he felt more outraged. He tried to make eye contact with the people, so they would know that he was on their side, that he just saw them as ordinary people. But none of them even looked up.

This war wasn't about taking over other countries, Dietrich realised. It was about wiping out the Jews, and everyone else who was different. By making them wear the star, Nazis were inviting ordinary people in the streets – even young boys and girls – to look down on the Jews and hate them. To want them to disappear.

How strange that the British considered all Germans to be Nazi enemies, Dietrich thought. These Jews were Germans too, and they had been suffering under the Nazis longer than anyone else.

1945

'I don't doubt your diplomatic skills,' the Matron said, 'but what good did the Bishop do in the end? If he had managed to secure some sort of support from the British government, perhaps we might have had more of Hitler's officers on our side, and Stauffenberg would have succeeded. Perhaps we'd be running Berlin, and Hitler would be ten feet under.'

'I know the man, and I'm sure he did all he could. But he told me even then that he was our one public ally in Britain, and he was ridiculed for it.'

'Do you suppose there's anyone still on our side out there?' the Matron asked helplessly.

'God is for us,' Dietrich told her. 'I know it's easy to doubt that when you look only at the terror and pain that surround us. Even the church has been taken over by the Nazis, and has failed the people. God is for us, but to see it, one must look not at Germany, not at the church, not at anybody else at all, but only at Jesus. Do you remember when Peter saw Jesus walking on the water, and came out to walk with Him? So long as he looked only at Jesus, all was well, no matter how fierce the storm around him. But when he looked down at the raging water and listened to the howling wind, then fear was too much for him, and he sank.'

'It's a very good lesson,' said the Matron glumly. 'Except that I can't look past this storm. I can't hear past the Nazis howling like the wind. I try to think about Jesus, but His stories sound like fairy tales compared to the horror all around me. Where do I find Him?'

'My dear lady, if I decide myself where I may find God, then I will always find a God who is like me in some way, who reflects me. But if God decides where I will find Him, then it will be in a place like this one – full of horrors and suffering. This place is the Cross of Christ.'[3] He leaned toward her. 'You see, He suffered for us there, so that He may also know our suffering here, today. He is with us through it, and He can bring us safely into that other life, with no more suffering and no more death. We will meet this Jesus if we look for Him at the foot of the Cross.'

---

3. This is a quote from a letter that Dietrich wrote to one of his brothers-in-law. In the same letter he said that he believed all answers were to be found in the Bible, and that 'one must only ask repeatedly, and a little humbly, to receive this answer.'

⤳ THE BEGINNING OF THE END ⤶

The Aristocrat came to join them: an old, dignified man still wearing, over his worn-out uniform, the medal called 'Pour le Merite' – the highest distinction a soldier could get in the Great War.

'Dr Bonhoeffer,' he said. 'I know your family, of course, but I don't believe we've had the pleasure of meeting – at least since you were a boy! You probably don't remember. I've been away so long.'

'How could I forget the general who was going all the way to China?' Dietrich smiled. 'It caught my imagination. I often thought of you there, wondering how you were getting on in the Forbidden City, and wishing I could ask what it was like.'

'For me, it was like coming home,' the Aristocrat replied. 'Of course, it took some years to get my Mandarin up to scratch, but everything about the Chinese – the manners, the discipline, the honour, the philosophy – suited me perfectly. I wished to stay when the war started, but Hitler's men threatened to sell my home and send my family to a concentration camp if I didn't come back.' He thoughtfully touched the medal. 'Honour is important to me, and there was no greater dishonour in my life than being forced to serve my country – when that meant serving Hitler.'

'You must have seen a great change in Germany when you came back.'

'You know, when I left all those years ago, Germany was not so very different from China. The most important things were honour, love of country, courtesy and generosity – at least among my circles. That included your family. It feels as if that Germany has gone, and so many of its finest people have gone too.'

'The war forced its way into our homes and families,' Dietrich agreed. 'We tried to keep things as much the same as possible, and yet things were often not what they seemed.'

1943

A pleasant evening in March, and some of the greatest minds in the German Resistance were gathered in the home of Dietrich's sister Ursula and her husband Rudiger, practising for a family talent show. Dr Dietrich Bonhoeffer, professor and spy, was playing the piano. Rudiger, another conspirator, was on violin. Hans Dohnanyi, keeper and manipulator of government intelligence, was singing in the choir. They were practising a hymn called 'Praise the Lord' to perform at their father's 75th birthday party later that week.

Dietrich played every note perfectly but not with much feeling, as if he were hurrying through the piece. His brother Klaus kept glancing at the clock. Christel kept glancing at Dohnanyi. Dohnanyi had one eye on the street, where his car was parked at the door.

'What's wrong with everyone tonight?' the youngest Bonhoeffer sister, Susanne, fretted. 'This is a big occasion – we can do better!'

'Susi's right,' Dietrich said, trying to summon some enthusiasm. 'There's a lot at stake. Let's play like we mean it. Praise the Lord – who knows what wonders He will do tonight!'

They sailed into the song again, but not really much better than before. The tension was stretched so tightly in the room that it felt as if something must shatter. With every hour that passed it seemed to strain more and more, until finally, just as the rehearsal finished, the telephone rang.

Dohnanyi made a move for it as if he couldn't help himself, even though it wasn't his house. Rudiger went to answer it instead. 'The Schleichers. Yes?'

He listened for a moment, said 'Thank you,' and hung up the phone again. He looked at Dohnanyi and gave a slight shake of his head.

'What's wrong?' Susanne whispered as she was leaving. 'You know I have some idea what you're all up to, Dietrich.'

'Everything went right,' he replied. 'Except the bomb didn't go off.'

'The bomb?'

'We were expecting a call to say the war was ended.' He shrugged. 'It turns out this is a day like any other.'

The plot they had been working on for months had failed. The day had come and gone. Hitler and the bomb had been in the right place, but not for long enough: he had left the building early. The man who was to set off the bomb managed to disarm it and no harm was done; the plot was not discovered. But Hitler was still alive to massacre his millions and rage against the world's armies. The war was not over.

'What do we do now, Dietrich?' Susanne asked.

'We celebrate Father's birthday,' he told her.

When the real celebration came along, the great minds of the Resistance played and sang rather better. There was no distraction now, no great hope, no great failure. The war went on, and they took the time to rejoice in one another in the midst of all the horror. The plot had failed but they sang 'Praise to the Lord, the Almighty, the King of Creation'.

At the end of the party, they welcomed a special visitor: a representative from Hitler himself, giving Karl Bonhoeffer a medal in recognition of his great work as an academic and psychologist. The family just about kept straight faces, knowing that no medal from a man as stupid as Hitler could mean anything to Karl Bonhoeffer. It was a good night, but for those in the know, it was impossible not to wonder how different the evening would have been if the plot had succeeded.

But it had not, and Dietrich's thoughts turned toward the future. Eberhard was about to get married to Rudiger and Ursula's daughter Renate, and he himself was secretly engaged too – though not even his family knew it yet! The next time the whole family gathered together would be at Eberhard's wedding, then at his own. Surely by then the war would be over. Even Gert and Sabine might be there, back from their exile in London! The future was not certain, but it was hopeful.

1945

'And do you still hope?' the Aristocrat asked.

'Every day. Even when hope is painful. How could we survive without hope?'

'Dear boy, of course we must cling to whatever we can, but Hitler himself is determined to snuff us out. It's unlikely we will all make it to the end of the war. Chinese philosophy has taught me to accept my fate with quiet resignation.'

Dietrich was quiet for a moment. Then he said, 'I've been thinking of writing a poem about a story from Exodus. No doubt you've read of Moses on Mount Nebo.'

'I know Moses, of course. I blush to admit I don't recall what happened on Mount Nebo.'

'Moses had led the children of Israel in the desert for forty years, and they had reached the very edge of the Promised Land. But Moses had disobeyed God, and his punishment was that he himself would not enter the land with them. However, God in His grace took Moses up to Mount Nebo, where he could see Canaan stretched out before him. He could not go there himself, but he could see the fields and vineyards and streams laid out before him and know that there his people would find rest.'[1]

The Aristocrat nodded. 'Perhaps, like the Chinese philosophers, he resigned himself to death, and therefore died with peace.'

Dietrich shook his head. 'He had a certain hope, knowing God was faithful. That was his peace.'

'Bonhoeffer, do you think we'll live to see the promised land?'

'I can see it from where I'm standing, General.'

---

1. Deuteronomy chapter 34.

∽ THE FEAST ∾

Just as Dietrich finished his story, the guards burst into the room. The Coward jumped. But the guards brought with them an unusually pleasant aroma.

'A gift from the village!' one of them cried. 'Bread and potato salad!'

More potatoes, yes, but how glad the prisoners were to see them. A real feast – not enough food, of course, for how could they ever again see enough food? – but it was so good. Not a word was spoken while they were all eating.

'Pastor!' one of them called out afterward. 'You got too excited about the potato salad – you didn't remind us to say grace.'

'We can thank God for the food after it's eaten instead of before,' he replied with a laugh.

The prisoners stood and bowed their heads, even the Nephew, who didn't believe in God. Everyone felt humbled and grateful before this almost miraculous provision.

'Oh God, you show your goodness to us even in this prison,' Dietrich prayed. 'Thank you for such mercy. Bless those who sent to us in our need and reward them as if they had fed your Son. Amen.'

The prisoners looked up smiling. Dietrich had a sudden flash of memory – the long dinners at his seminaries, the hymns and prayers and sermons and discussions that had accompanied the simple food. Food nearly as simple as this, though rather more plentiful.

Now, too, there was lazy conversation: what else was there to do in the short evening before lights out?

The Nephew was looking particularly despondent tonight, sitting alone on his bed whilst the other prisoners were milling around and chatting.

Dietrich was trying to get some reading done when the Blonde came up to him with a peculiar, too-wide smile and perched on the edge of his bed. 'Laugh,' she said. 'Don't ask why, just do it.'

He merely gave her a confused smile. 'I'm sorry, it's been a while since I've done any acting. What's going on?'

She clucked at him. 'That Russian boy's in love with me. I'm just letting him know he's not the only one.'

Dietrich raised his eyebrows. 'Is that why he's so sad tonight, because you're going around making eyes at the other men? Vassily's a sweet boy. You don't like him?'

'Oh yes, I do, but I don't want him to know it yet. I want to keep things interesting for a while.'

'Things are interesting enough in here. Why not make him happy, and let him know you like him too?'

'Things aren't interesting at all in here. Nothing ever happens, it's just boring all the time. I was prepared for torture, cruelty, and starvation, but not for the utter boredom.'

'I admit time can move slowly,' Dietrich said. 'But we're in a good place here. At least we've got a bit more freedom and comfort.'

'I just feel like I have more time to think about how hungry I am and whether I did the right thing getting myself into this trouble in the first place.'

'You think you shouldn't have worked against Hitler?'

'I think I did very little good, and now I'm stuck. It's all so meaningless. Don't you ever wonder if there was any point to what you did?'

He shrugged. 'The fight against Hitler is so much bigger than my being inconvenienced by prison. I wish I'd been able to do more – but not because I'm in here. Because Hitler's still out there.'

'Well, I don't claim to understand the bigger picture the way you do. All I know is I'm sick of this! I'm sick of starving and freezing and the same faces and the same room and' – suddenly she was almost shouting – 'and sometimes I think I can't take it anymore! Don't you ever feel that?'

'Yes, I do.' He was quiet for a moment, considering. 'But I am not surprised by it. Anyone who takes part in a great fight, like we did, has to count the cost. Certainly nobody stands against the Fuhrer without knowing it's a death sentence.'

'Knowing it is one thing, and living it is another. Don't tell me your heart didn't sink when you saw the Gestapo at your door.'

'Of course it did. But I was ready. I had been for years.'

1943

Five days after Karl Bonhoeffer's magnificent birthday party, Dietrich was working in his study. The Nazi government had forbidden him to publish any more books – his short volume on the Psalms was, they had decided, pro-Jew, and he must be punished for that – but he knew they wouldn't be in power forever. This book would take a long time to write, and by the time it was finished, surely he'd be able to publish again. It was called Ethics: a study of a most appropriate field, from a Christian point of view. It was something Dietrich needed to write about. Every Christian was having trouble finding the right way to follow God in this horrible war, as the young Werner had demonstrated. Dietrich had seen churches make decisions that went against the Bible, and fail to stand up for those who were suffering, and even allow themselves to be used by the Nazis. He was starting to dream of a kind of Christianity that didn't depend on the rules of a church, but only on people's relationship with God and His Word. Jesus had described it as 'worshipping the Father in spirit and in truth.' And the closer people got to God and His Word, the better they would get at knowing right from wrong.

Dietrich finished a couple hours of fierce writing and then realised he was hungry. It was already lunchtime. But before taking a break, he decided to call Hans von Dohnanyi and ask if he was needed to travel anywhere that week. If not, he had a good solid chunk of time to work on his book.

He picked up the phone and gave the operator Dohnanyi's number. The phone rang several times and then clicked into life. 'Hello?'

It was a man's voice but not Hans'. A stranger. Dietrich slammed the receiver down.

He slipped quickly out of the house and into the garden next door, where Ursula and Rudiger lived.

He found his sister in the kitchen, cooking bratwurst for lunch. She stopped, spoon in hand, when she saw how pale he was.

'Dietrich! What's wrong?'

Although white, he was perfectly calm. 'It's Hans and Christel. I just rang their house, and a strange man answered.'

Ursula went as white as Dietrich. 'The Gestapo.'

'You'll have to tell Rudiger to be careful; he's implicated too. You understand they'll come for me next. Make sure everyone knows what to answer to any questions they might be asked.'

She nodded. 'You're just working with Hans. You're a simple pastor and you don't know about any wider resistance. None of us knows anything.'

'I hate leaving Hans to take the blame for everything when I've supported him in all he's done.'

'Hans will be fine. He's one of the best legal minds in the country – he can defend himself. And he really is far more involved than you. What's important is that as much of the family survives as possible.'

'I might not get much to eat in prison. Do you have a sausage to spare?'

'Dietrich! How can you think of your stomach at a time like this, when you're about to be arrested by those thugs?'

'God has my fate in His hands. I can't change anything by worrying. I should do what I can to keep well, and eating lunch will help. You don't mind, do you?'

'Mind? Everything in the kitchen is yours.'

He laughed. 'I don't think I could eat that much!'

'It'll be ready in fifteen minutes.'

Dietrich went back to his parents' home and set his papers in order. Mother and Father must be able to find his things. Perhaps they could bring him his work on Ethics in prison once he was able to receive visitors. He checked again to make sure there was no evidence of his work in the Resistance, and even left a few notes that would put the Gestapo on the wrong track. On his way out of the house, he saw his mother getting ready to go out. He was glad: she wouldn't be there when the police came. She didn't know yet that Hans and Christel were in prison. He went and hugged her and arranged her scarf more comfortably.

'You look nice, Mama,' he said.

She smiled. 'You haven't called me that since you were a child.'

'Haven't I? I don't know what came over me.' He kissed her cheek. 'I'm going to Ursula's for lunch. See you later.'

'At dinner,' she replied on her way out the door. He didn't answer.

Back at Ursula's house Dietrich sat and ate the bratwurst with sauerkraut, talking to his sister, and looking around her familiar kitchen. Strange to think that he wouldn't be seeing it for a while. Surely it wouldn't be that long, though – not with his powerful connections, not with Hans von Dohnanyi directing their case. Not with Maria waiting for him.

At 4:00 his father appeared in the kitchen. 'Dietrich,' he said. 'There are two gentlemen who wish to speak with you. They're in your room – and not by invitation.'

'I'm coming.' He kissed his sister and followed his father outside. Once in the garden, he shook his hand tightly. 'Hans and Christel are already away, Papa.

I didn't want to worry you, but I suppose now you need to know. Ask Mama to pray for me. Especially when I'm questioned.'

'You'll do well, Dietrich. God will be with you.' Karl's voice was calm but there were tears standing in his eyes. Though he did not believe in God, he had never mocked his son's or wife's faith, and now he simply seemed glad they had it.

Up in Dietrich's room, two men in officers' uniforms were busy rifling through his writing desk, stuffing any papers that interested them into a satchel. 'Dietrich Bonhoeffer,' the older one said, 'you are under arrest. You'll come with us to Tegel.'

Karl groaned. It was hard to hear that his dear youngest son was going to prison. But there was nothing he could do.

'It's all right, Father,' Dietrich said. 'I'm happy to help these men with their enquiries. I have nothing to hide. May I take one thing, gentlemen?' He picked up his brother Walter's Bible. 'Now I'm at your service.'

1945

'Part of me thought I'd be out within weeks, if not days,' Dietrich said. 'First I thought I'd be able to go to Eberhard and Renate's wedding a month later. Then maybe for Christmas. Then for their child's christening – they named him after me. The most I could do was send a letter with my blessing; I even sent a sermon to be read out for the christening! You have not been in prison as long as me, Fraulein, but already you must know how people's lives go on without you. For a while I thought

I really couldn't bear it. I was afraid I'd be killed on some officer's whim. I even wondered if it would be better to kill myself so I couldn't give up any secrets under torture.'

She nodded. 'I thought about taking that route. It's such a shock to be in prison that it sends you into despair. How did you get out of it?'

'I remembered something important. I told you I had counted the cost when I joined the Resistance, but long before that, I'd also counted the cost when I became a Christian. Jesus said that the cost of following Him is our life – it no longer belongs to us, but to Him. My life was not mine to throw away.'

⤳ THE MATRON ⤶

Dietrich was standing at the window, watching the sunset. What a glorious light, all pink and purple painted above the dark outline of the forest. Despite being in prison, he felt like a rich man when he owned this view.

'Beautiful, isn't it?' said the Matron, smiling beside him. 'I never took you for much of a romantic, Pastor Bonhoeffer.'

'Oh, I'm just enjoying God's handiwork,' he replied. 'Though I fear my fiancée would agree with you – she said herself I wasn't romantic.'

'You are engaged!'

'Yes. It was secret – she was so young that her mother asked us to wait a year and not tell anyone. Even my family didn't know until after I was arrested. We had our first and only kiss in a prison cell, with my guard watching. Of course, it's hard to be romantic under those circumstances.'

1943

In prison in Berlin, Dietrich felt as if he were doing three kinds of waiting at once. Waiting for things he knew would happen at certain times, like lights out; things he expected to happen but had no idea when, like his family's visits; and things he could only hope for, like freedom.

'A visitor for you, Bonhoeffer,' said the Captain.

It must be Father, or one of his brothers. Or maybe it could be Eberhard on leave from Italy. Perhaps he would have brought a few clothes and books and some extra food! He followed the Captain down to the visitation room, a cell with cheap carpet tacked on the floor, a chair for the guard to supervise the visit, and a worn-out two-seat sofa. The little table in front of the sofa left barely enough room for the prisoner and the visitor to stand up at the same time.

The Captain bundled Dietrich into the room. 'Fraulein von Wedermeyer will be in in a minute, Bonhoeffer. Rather young and not ugly. You've done well there, you old dog!' He winked.

Dietrich didn't even have time to resent the officer's teasing tone. He stood still, his mouth open. He was to see Maria like this, dressed in his shabbiest clothes, no preparation, no warning? She had come here?

And there she was, a breath of clear mountain air in her traditional dirndl blouse and full skirt with modern, pretty shoes and hat and handbag. Her smile was shy, nervous, but contagious. Over her arm was a huge basket of clothes, books, cakes, real ground coffee, and ever so much more.

'Maria,' he said wonderingly.

'Pastor Bonhoeffer,' she replied, and then she burst out laughing. 'I'm more bold in my letters than in person! I suppose I should call you Dietrich now.'

'You should certainly start before we get married,' he said, smiling.

She held up her basket. 'An engagement gift. Though not much of a gift – all your own things! Well, perhaps there's a new book or two from me, and one or two delicious things from our farm.'

He didn't even glance at the basket. He couldn't take his eyes from her face. 'I can't believe you're here. How sorry I am that you have to come into this place. You should never have seen inside these walls. And seeing me like this' – he looked down at his drab, rumpled shirt, baggy on him after a few months of prison fare.

'I intend to see you in all conditions, for better and for worse,' she reminded him. 'I hope you don't mind, but we can't have a secret engagement anymore. My applying for a fiancée pass to see you rather let the cat out of the bag.'

'You can shout it from the rooftops if you want,' he smiled.

'I do want. I still can't quite believe that a genius like you should marry someone so inexperienced and ordinary as me. Before you, I hadn't even met anyone who'd been to America! I'm still rather puzzled why you should want me. But you do, don't you?'

'Nothing is more natural than a man loving a woman who is young and beautiful. As for inexperience – well, let's just say we have much to discuss. So many books, and places to see, and' –

'And theology,' she said, laughing. 'I've been trying to make my way through your book *Discipleship*, but I keep falling asleep. It's a lovely sleep, it makes me dream of you!'

'If you can sleep well, darling, I'm glad my book is good for something.'

'But Dietrich' – she blushed – 'are you quite sure about me? You don't realise how silly I can be. Sometimes I'm quite theatrical.'

'I shall love nothing more than to share your adventures with you,' he returned, and then became serious. 'When you wrote to me your "yes," Maria, all those months ago, I was afraid you accepted me because your grandmother approved, or maybe because your mother didn't! But now that you're here, I can see you really do love me – don't you?'

She blushed and nodded.

'Five minutes,' said the guard.

'You're real,' Maria said. 'I've hardly believed it for months, knowing I had a fiancé but never setting eyes on him since our engagement.'

'You're real,' he said. 'There's a world outside this prison.' He took her hand. 'Promise me you won't worry.'

'I can't promise that. Of course I'll worry. My whole world is in here. Dietrich, I worry all the time about you, every minute.'

'But I'm not worried. Not about what will happen to me. Make your worries into prayers. And promise me you'll keep your health, whatever happens. You won't wear yourself out working, or trying to help me from the outside.'

'I'll sit and do needlework like a lady, nothing else.'

'Plan the wedding. Pick out furniture. Design some wallpaper.'

'You'll laugh when I tell you that everything is already fixed: what flowers are to be on the table when you come for the wedding, which room you're to sleep in, what book is to be lying on your bedside table and what picture hanging above it, what order the bridesmaids and ushers are to walk in, and who is to make what speeches. I always feel rather as if I were telling a fairy tale, but lots of fairy tales come true, so why shouldn't ours?'[1]

They smiled at each other rather sadly.

'Do write,' he said.

'I do. Every day. On days I can't come to the post office I write to you in my journal.'

'I can send you a letter every ten days. Maybe more, if they decide I've been on good behaviour. I've already been promoted to using a knife and fork again with all my meals, so who knows.'

'What were you using, chopsticks?'

'Apparently prisoners can't be trusted with cutlery. I'd almost forgotten how to eat with it. It's very funny how little one minds about such things – well, perhaps not everyone.'

'You'll have to be reintroduced to civilisation again when you get out.'

'Your visits will help. They'll remind me there's a reason to stay civilised.'

'One minute,' said the guard.

'Oh, Dietrich, already!' Maria cried. 'Isn't it a little bit cruel? That God only brought us together so recently, and we never even got to meet as an engaged couple before you came in here? It feels like a curse.'

'Maria, you are nothing but a blessing. An evidence of God's nearness and favour. I don't know how I'd get through each day without knowing that you're out there, praying for me, and loving me.'

---

1. Maria really said this. In her letters, she wrote him all the details she had planned out for their wedding and their new home together.

The guard stood up.

'Every morning at six,' she said hurriedly. 'I read the Scriptures for the day and I pray for you. If you're awake' –

'Yes, darling, yes. We'll be praying for each other, together but apart.'

'Tomorrow then,' she said, with a bright smile.

'Tomorrow,' he said. And she was gone, but she seemed to leave a glow behind.

1945

'Do you know,' Dietrich said, 'that Christmas, she showed up at the prison with an enormous Christmas tree? It was so large it couldn't fit inside my cell – at least if I was to keep my bed – so they had to put it in the guards' room instead. And what a cheer it was to them, to have a bit of Christmas in that place. To feel that they, too, could await and celebrate the coming of the Christ child.'

'Doesn't it feel sometimes, in this war, that the waiting is the eternal thing, and the end never in sight?' the Matron sighed.

'Do you know why Advent, the waiting, is so important? It reminds that we are now waiting for Christ to come back. And sometimes it seems to me that the worse things get, the closer I feel His return. I feel now that all my waiting, whether it's for my freedom or my wedding, has all become part of my waiting for Christ. After all, only He can really fulfil all these longings.'

'Pastor Bonhoeffer, I wish I had your faith.'

'Dear lady, you can. All you need is to ask for it.'

ꙍ EWIGKEIT ꙍ

Finally the chatting died down and the room was filled with the deep breathing of thirteen sleepers. Dietrich lay awake, his eyes wide open in the darkness. He could hear the Nephew's quiet snores a few feet away, and he imagined that instead it was his twin sister Sabine. He was ten years old again, surrounded not by a strange dormitory and other prisoners, but his parents' familiar heavy furniture, intricately carved, and the faint scent of his mother's perfume.

'Ewigkeit', Dietrich would say, and Sabine would murmur the word after him. It was like the start of a religious ritual. It meant *eternity*. Together in silence they would muse on the word; in the dark, it had an almost eerie sound. Trying to imagine true endlessness, they would feel awed, dizzy, almost sick at the enormousness of it. In comparison they felt tiny, as small as eternity was huge.

He wondered if Sabine was still thinking about eternity now, in her new life in London. Maybe she talked about it sometimes with Gert. He had not seen Sabine for – how many years now? Five, six? He remembered driving them to the Swiss border, the night they had escaped Germany, and how quiet the car had seemed, driving back without them.

Prison life sometimes felt like eternity, an endless run of days stretching out into the distance; so, too, did war. Both of these things seemed to be drawing near the end, and yet the end never seemed quite to come.

Frightening as it was – the idea of unendingness – much scarier was the idea of an end, a real permanent end. Perhaps that was really why he had become a theologian, Dietrich thought: to prove that there could be eternal life. For him, for Sabine, for Walter.

Eternity had always seemed terrifying until that first summer in New York, when Dietrich saw the real love of Jesus and gave Himself over to it. Now it seemed like a haven to reach, an endless supply of hours to spend with his beloved Jesus, not at all the shapeless dark thing that he had always imagined. Funny, how there were fewer and fewer things to fear as he grew older. He used to fear death. Before he was arrested, he had feared torture, and had feared he would give away other people's secrets in the midst of it. Now he knew that God had always given him strength just in the moment he needed it, and that He always would.

He thought of God sending the Israelites manna to eat in the wilderness. They were only allowed to gather enough each morning for that day, and they had to trust that God would provide more the next day. In the same way, Dietrich had found that he couldn't store up the courage and strength he needed for the time ahead – but he had learned that God would always give it to him for each new trial. That was how Jesus kept Dietrich depending only on Him, and not on his own strength or cleverness.

So, whether in his own tiny lone cell in the Berlin prison, or in this big new room full of near-strangers, Dietrich could give thanks and fall asleep in peace, no matter what tomorrow brought.

* * *

It was still dark when Dietrich was woken – not by the guards banging into the room, or the beds collapsing, but by a gentle shaking on his shoulder.

'Yes?' he asked, sitting up and fumbling for his glasses, not that he could see much by the faint moonlight. 'Who is it?'

'It's me – Rascher.'

'Doctor. What's the matter?'

'I couldn't sleep.'

'Was it something I said?'

'Not exactly. I just wanted to clear something up. I think you've got the wrong impression of me, Bonhoeffer. You seem to think I'm under some kind of wrath. You know I'm a Christian, don't you? I'm baptised and confirmed. I'm a good husband, father, citizen. Why are you siding with Jews before fellow Christians?'

'What God do you believe in? The God of the Bible, or one made up by Hitler?'

Rascher didn't answer. He just said, 'Jesus was killed by the Jews!'

'Jesus was a Jew. He was killed by all those who do wrong. He sacrificed Himself to pay the price for our sins.'

'What do my sins have to do with a random carpenter who got Himself crucified?' There was a sneer in Rascher's voice.

'Nothing, unless you believe He is God.'

'So your God Himself is a Jew. That explains a lot.'

'Rascher, if you went through confirmation classes, you know all of these things – even if the Nazis have tried to rewrite the Bible. Did you wake me up just to scoff at my faith?'

'No. I respect you, Bonhoeffer. You are an educated and perceptive and pleasant fellow. In another time and place, we might have been friends.'

'Certainly, Doctor. I've enjoyed your company too.'

'I've kept the prisoners laughing. I've stood up to the guards when necessary. I've shared whatever information I had from my access to the higher levels of Nazi command.'

'Yes.'

'In short, I've been a nice guy.'

'Absolutely.'

'So why the insistence that your God – who may or may not be more real than my more nationalistic God – wants to send me to an eternity of judgment?'

Bonhoeffer was quiet for a moment. 'Rascher, everyone here is under God's judgment. Me included. The only difference is what your defence will be. Are you going to plead the blood of that Jew, Jesus, or are you going to insist that being decent to your fellow prisoners will grant you heaven?'

'I don't know if I even believe in heaven. I just take offence that you want to send me to the other place.'

'Do you believe in the other place?'

126

'It makes very little difference what I think,' Rascher shot back. 'The point is, I've been judged unfairly by the country I love, and now you think I'll get the same treatment after I die!'

'Tell me, what did you get arrested for?'

Rascher let out a ragged sigh. Finally he said, 'Loving too much.'

Dietrich smiled at that. 'You're going to have to be more specific.'

'One of my scientific aims was to make people more productive in having children. There was a pressure for me and my wife to demonstrate it. So we acquired more children in, well, whatever way we could.'

'You adopted some?'

'Yes, exactly! Only the government decided to use uglier words – buying. Even kidnapping. But you see, once those children were in our family, we loved them as our own. We raised them far better than their parents could have done.'

'So the government was wrong to call you to account for it?'

'Let's just say they could have taken a more reasoned view.'

'Rascher, is there anything in your whole life that you feel genuinely sorry about?'

'There are things I could have done better.'

'No. I mean things that you know you did wrong. That you feel guilty for.'

'I've always been an upstanding citizen. I have no regrets.'

'Then there is no place for you in God's Kingdom. You clearly have no need for Jesus' forgiveness – and

He can only have fellowship with those He has washed and forgiven. When I was younger, I was obsessed with the Sermon on the Mount. I wrote a study of it and published it as a book called *The Cost of Discipleship*. I'll summarise the book for you: when you say you can know God without repentance – without turning away from the wrong things you do – you're saying Christ's death wasn't necessary. That's cheap grace. But real grace is expensive; it cost the life of God's Son. So there can be no forgiveness without repentance. Repentance and humility are the only way to know God. And you, Rascher, can still repent.'

'So your God demands weakness? Well then, I think I'd rather be a good German than a good Christian.' Rascher stormed away.

Ewigkeit. Now Dietrich remembered why the word had sounded so sinister. An eternity without God was a picture of true horror.

∽ ESCAPE ∽

There was not much sleep after his late-night talk with Rascher, but Dietrich was up at dawn again for his 6 a.m. appointment with Maria. Him with his Bible, her with her Bible – somewhere. Their verses for the day were about Jesus' sacrifice and resurrection. Jesus felt especially close to Dietrich that morning, as if He were physically in the room. As if He too were just sitting with the prisoners, waiting for something. Or someone.

All this waiting, Dietrich thought. We've been waiting not just throughout this war but from the moment Adam and Eve were cast out of Eden. First waiting for the Saviour to come; now waiting for Him to come back again. That's the only thing really worth waiting for.

The others were up now, and the Wolf appeared beside him with a mug of peppermint tea. 'We had to reuse the leaves,' he said. 'I hope there's still some kind of taste in there.'

Dietrich smiled at him. 'You're very kind.'

'You really are a funny chap,' the Wolf laughed. 'You're positively radiating contentment over a cup of lukewarm water with a few specks in it.'

'Do you ever get the feeling that prison is just a dream? That really we could just walk out of here and run into the forest and no one would mind?'

'Probably we could at this stage, old boy. The guards might shoot a few bullets for the sake of it, but nobody would make a big fuss. Still, I wouldn't advise it – the war will end any day, and then we'll be set free without any risk to life or limb.'

'Oh, I was just thinking that, in some strange way, I feel free this morning. I'm not entertaining any idea of escape – not anymore.'

'You did before? Most of us do, I suppose, but I never had a solid plan.'

'A year ago,' Dietrich said, 'I practically had one foot out the door.'

1944

Tomorrow would be the day.

With every passing moment, Dietrich thought: only one more day in Tegel Prison. Only one more time before I'm free. One more breakfast of stale bread and lard and fake coffee. One more five-minute shower in that filthy bathroom shared by so many. One more exercise walking around and around the garden. One more night, one more morning. Then –

He exchanged a glance with his guard, Knoblauch, through the little window in his door. Both men's breathing quickened and they quickly looked away. Best to keep their attention here. Be cheerful. Be attentive. Be witty and thoughtful. Complain as if you were expecting another two years in this cell, in this job. Beg for more food as if you don't know when you'll get your next meal. And all the while, live and breathe the plan.

The previous night Knoblauch had gone to Ursula under cover of darkness to collect a mechanic's uniform and ration coupons for him.

This day Knoblauch would smuggle Dietrich that uniform.

The following day they would simply walk out of the prison together at the end of Knoblauch's shift.

In the woods Dietrich would get into his own clothes. Then …

Switzerland. Freedom. They'd make it to Karl Barth and Dietrich's other friends. Wait out the war. Marry Maria. Rebuild the country. Out of jail, over the border, and into the future.

Knoblauch was risking more, really. He was doing all right for himself. Not that he enjoyed guarding prisoners at Tegel, but he wasn't in trouble. Dietrich was in jail anyway, his life in danger; why not run? But he and Knoblauch didn't have time for long discussions about why they each wanted to escape. Knoblauch must have his own reasons, Dietrich supposed. All he had said was, 'A man like you should not be in here. I'll help you.'

Nothing to do but wait. The hours passed quickly and contentedly as Dietrich thought about what he'd do outside these walls. He'd feel the peace of the forest around him, the rustling of leaves, the rushing of a stream, the smell of earth and plants and flowers instead of cement and cabbage soup and unwashed prisoners. Even if he had to sleep in the garden shed Knoblauch kept at the edge of the city, he'd sleep in peace, with no screams in the next room, no guard banging his door open at 5.30 a.m. for shower time. In Switzerland he'd eat pastries and chocolate and coffee and spaghetti and veal, glistening with fat, with fluffy potatoes and fresh green vegetables and good wine and good conversation.

At lunchtime Knoblauch brought his lunch tray and a bundle.

Dietrich wolfed down his lunch almost without noticing it – nothing more than a small bowl of thin soup and a little black bread. But he took the bundle of clothes as if it were made of gold. This was his freedom.

Knoblauch started to say something; then one of his superior officers called his name, and he gave Dietrich a serious look before closing the cell door.

Dietrich retreated to the corner of his cell, turned away from the door, and opened the bundle carefully, shielding it with his body in case someone came in again.

The mechanic's outfit was there. So were the coupons. And so was a note, in Ursula's handwriting: 'The files are discovered. Klaus has been arrested.'

Their brother Klaus.

The files.

The files, 'The Chronicle of Shame.' Dohnanyi had kept the records since 1938 on Canaris' orders. They contained evidence of every illegal activity, every brutality, every crime against humanity, that the Nazis had carried out. The files were aimed at exposing them before the world and punishing them when the war was over and the regime defeated. Only enemies of the state could have kept those files. Dietrich's family were now enemies of the state.

Knoblauch finally got a few minutes in Dietrich's cell at dinner time.

'Canaris, the head of the Abwehr – is there any news of him?' Dietrich asked.

'Arrested. So is everyone that worked under him, or had anything to do with him. Your brother Klaus is now in prison and things look much worse for Dohnanyi. If he wasn't facing a death sentence before, he probably is now. Hitler is furious. It may be wiser if we go today. Now. Are you ready? To put on your mechanic's clothes will take only a moment.'

Dietrich looked at the bundle from home. All he had to do was slip it on over his clothes, fold his ration coupons into the pocket, and hide his Bible in Knoblauch's bag. He would be free.

Or would he?

'Free to hide,' he muttered to himself. 'Free, myself, but putting those I love in danger. Free, but always looking over my shoulder for the Gestapo to come after me.'

'What?'

Dietrich looked up. 'I've run away before, Knoblauch. But God brought me back. I was afraid of suffering with my people, but He told me it was where He wanted me.'

'Please, sir, think. You are implicated in Canaris' and Dohnanyi's work. The files they kept against Hitler. The Jews they helped to escape. The plots to harm the Fuhrer. Pastor, this may be your last chance to get away.'

'Do you realise that if I escape, it makes everyone connected with me look more guilty? They'd arrest others in my family. Perhaps my fiancée. It would make things worse for Klaus and Dohnanyi and anyone else they're already investigating. And there's no certainty even of getting me out of Germany.'

Knoblauch looked down. 'I thought perhaps, if I could save one man like you, I would have done one significant thing in my life.'

Dietrich laid a hand on the man's slumped shoulder. 'I'll never forget this, my friend. But I can't run from God's will. Only He can save me.'

1945

'You were right not to run,' the Wolf said. 'You'd never have got out of Germany. And now you're practically staring freedom in the face.'

'You know, today, I feel as if I am,' Dietrich said cheerfully.

❧ CHURCH ❧

'I understand we have a very valuable resource at our disposal,' the Matron called out when she saw Dietrich was awake.

'And what is that?' he asked.

'You, Pastor Bonhoeffer. It's Sunday, and we have one of Germany's best preachers. Shouldn't we benefit?'

'Yes, we are all sharing what we have, old man,' said the Wolf. 'It will be most stingy if you refuse to share your talents.'

'I am perfectly happy to do what I can,' Dietrich replied. 'But I am not willing to impose myself on anyone. My friend Dr Punder (here he nodded at a man whom Rascher had dubbed the Statesman) is a Catholic – I know that some others of you are, too. Perhaps not all will not want to hear Protestant preaching.'

'My dear Bonhoeffer,' the Statesman replied, 'I dare say anyone who believes in God, and His Son Jesus Christ, would benefit from your ministry.'

'I'm glad you think so,' Dietrich replied, 'but at least one of us, our Russian friend, does not believe in God

– and if we hold a service, having only this one room, it will be impossible for him to escape from it.'

'It is most kind you think of me,' said the Nephew, 'but have I not been willing to listen to you tell of your God? I will like very much to hear how you speak of Him to other Christians.'

Rascher did not add his voice to the general clamour for Dietrich to speak, but he didn't protest either. He just looked away sulkily.

'Very well,' said Dietrich. 'In an hour I will gladly speak to you all.'

* * *

The other prisoners formed a makeshift church. There were no chairs in the room, only beds, so they sat on the floor. Ragged they looked too, in their bits and pieces of clothes and uniforms and items from the Wolf's wardrobe. They looked like the Bonhoeffer children playing church, many years before, listening to their brother pretend to preach. They looked as a group of Jewish peasants might have looked, sitting on the ground to listen to Jesus give the Sermon on the Mount.

Dietrich opened his book of daily Bible readings for the German church and read them out.

But he was pierced for our transgressions, he was crushed for our iniquities; the punishment that brought us peace was on him, and by his wounds we are healed (Isa. 53:5).

Blessed be the God and Father of our Lord Jesus Christ!
By his great mercy we have been born anew to a living
hope through the resurrection of Jesus Christ from the
dead (1 Peter 1:3 RSV).

Dietrich raised his face and smiled at the twelve faces in front of him.

'I haven't told many of you about Maria. She used to visit me often when I was still held at Tegel Prison in Berlin. Of course it would take a long time for our letters to get to one another, sometimes weeks – sometimes never. In one of her letters she said that every morning she woke with the thought "Perhaps today is the day!" She thought that day might bring the news of my release. Or the end of the war. Or the death of Hitler. Or, because our letters took so long, it could be that she would simply turn round that day and find me standing behind her, already out of prison and across the country. She was looking forward to a day of freedom, and a day of peace from war, and a day when we would finally celebrate our marriage. You see, Maria is my fiancée. Now neither of us knows where the other is, but every morning I still think to myself, "Perhaps today is the day!"'

'We have each been in prison for a long time. Some of us' – nodding at the Wolf – 'longer than others. Some of us have struggled to continue hoping that the day of freedom and peace will ever arrive. Some of us have become accustomed to walking with death. Fear has overtaken hope, so that when we think "Today is the day," we mean "Perhaps today is the day I die."'

'Well, perhaps it is, for any one of us. Yet we need not fear. How do we know that dying is so dreadful? Who knows whether, in our human fear and anguish, we are only shivering and shuddering at the most glorious, heavenly, blessed event in the world?

'This is, of course, what Jesus has done for us: His resurrection not only delivers us from death, but the promise of eternal life delivers us from the very fear of death. No one has yet believed in God and the kingdom of God, and not been homesick from that hour, waiting and looking forward joyfully to being released from bodily existence.

'So, perhaps this is the day. The day that we go home, one way or another. Home to our families, or home to our God – which should we choose? And the fact is, if we are free from fear, we are free indeed. I look around at this weary group and I see men and women whose bodies are in prison, but whose souls may, if they only cast their lot with Christ who suffered for them, soar above every threat and cruelty. Jesus put Himself in the power of the men He created so that all those who believe in Him might never be under anyone's power again.

'This is the day. This is the day that the Lord has made. I will rejoice and be glad in it.'

Dietrich led the congregation in his high powerful voice, singing the great hymn of Luther, the preacher of the German people: 'A Mighty Fortress is Our God'. Then he raised his hands for the final prayer. 'Now to him who can keep you from falling …'

Even before he finished the blessing, the door clattered open. Two men marched into the room. They were not in uniform, but it was obvious from their straight bearing, their cold, hard faces, and the air of authority with which they walked in on the meeting: they were officers. 'Prisoner Bonhoeffer,' said one of them. 'Get ready to come with us.'

Everyone knew what those words meant.

Dietrich gave them a slow nod and turned to look at his friends. On the Nephew's face was despair, on the Wolf's sympathy, tears in the Bombshell's eyes, resignation in the Aristocrat's, fury in the Matron's, and in Rascher's, a terrible emptiness.

Dietrich reached out and grasped his friends' hands. His own face was the only one that bore no tears, no wrinkle of sorrow or pity. 'Remember me to our friend George Bell,' he said to the Wolf.

'I certainly will, if I get out of here. But what beastly bad luck for you. I was starting to hope we might hold out to the end of the war. Perhaps it isn't what we think after all – perhaps they're just moving you.'

Dietrich shook his head. 'This is the end,' he said, then smiled. 'But for me, the beginning of life.[1]'

---

1. Found in *The Venlo Incident*, these are the last recorded words of Dietrich Bonhoeffer.

∽ EPILOGUE ↝

When World War II finally ended, with Russian and American troops liberating Berlin, Germany was a ruin. There was little transportation, postal service, or telephone wires. But the German people were finally allowed to listen to radio stations from abroad. It was from the BBC that Dietrich Bonhoeffer's parents learned that he had been hanged at the Flossenberg extermination camp the morning after he'd left his schoolhouse jail. They listened to the broadcast of his memorial service, held at a London church he had pastored for a year.

It wasn't until later that they found out his brother Klaus and brothers-in-law Rudiger Schleicher and Hans von Dohnanyi were executed around the same time. Hitler had given orders to kill all those involved with Wilhelm Canaris' Resistance group, which Dohnanyi had helped run.

Eberhard Bethge made it through the war and wrote an enormous biography of his best friend. Maria went to America to study and to grieve, and married another theologian.

After many failed attempts by the German Resistance to kill Hitler, he finally committed suicide as Berlin fell to the Allied forces. His body was found by the Russians.

I first heard of Dietrich Bonhoeffer through a series of articles in *The Record*, the magazine of the Free Church of Scotland, written by Rev. Nigel Anderson. There was a certain glamour in the idea of a pastor who had plotted to kill Hitler, but I was also struck by the intelligence, quiet courage, and complexity of this German theologian. He was a complicated human being – far from perfect, but much more interesting for that! I certainly wanted to know more, so I very much enjoyed the research.

In writing this book I leaned heavily on *The Venlo Incident*, written by Payne Best ('the Wolf' in this book), as well as the biographies of Bonhoeffer by Eberhard Bethge, Charles Marsh, and Eric Metaxas. I also read parts of Bonhoeffer's books: *The Cost of Discipleship*, *Life Together*, *Love Letters from Cell 92*, and various essays. While some of the conversations here are imagined, they are all based closely on stories we know about Bonhoeffer and quotes from him.

I began writing this book just after the birth of my son Sorley, and finished it as he had his first birthday. 2017 was the year of Sorley and Bonhoeffer, and it seems entirely fitting that they should have occupied the same time – for what a wonderful role model Dietrich is, and what a wonderful way to think about how I would like my son to be. I hope he will grow into a man with Dietrich's childlike faith, submission to God, courage in the face of persecution, and most of all, finding in Jesus his refuge and fulfilment. And this is what I hope for all of my readers, and for you, too!

Christian Focus Publications

Our mission statement –

STAYING FAITHFUL

In dependence upon God we seek to impact the world through literature faithful to His infallible Word, the Bible. Our aim is to ensure that the Lord Jesus Christ is presented as the only hope to obtain forgiveness of sin, live a useful life and look forward to heaven with Him.

Our Books are published in four imprints:

CHRISTIAN FOCUS

popular works including biographies, commentaries, basic doctrine and Christian living.

CHRISTIAN HERITAGE

books representing some of the best material from the rich heritage of the church.

MENTOR

books written at a level suitable for Bible College and seminary students, pastors, and other serious readers. The imprint includes commentaries, doctrinal studies, examination of current issues and church history.

CF4•K

children's books for quality Bible teaching and for all age groups: Sunday school curriculum, puzzle and activity books; personal and family devotional titles, biographies and inspirational stories – Because you are never too young to know Jesus!

Christian Focus Publications Ltd,
Geanies House, Fearn, Ross-shire,
IV20 1TW, Scotland, United Kingdom.
www.christianfocus.com